AYRTON SENNA

By ALAN HENRY

PHOTOGRAPHS BY

AUTOSPORT PHOTOGRAPHIC

JEFF BLOXHAM

DIANA BURNETT

PAUL-HENRI CAHIER

COLORSPORT

LUKAS GORYS

INTERNATIONAL PRESS AGENCY

CHARLES BRISCOE-KNIGHT

NIGEL SNOWDON

OTHER TITLES IN THIS SERIES

Nigel Mansell
Niki Lauda
Alain Prost
Gilles Villeneuve
Emerson Fittipaldi
Jochen Rindt
Nelson Piquet
Jim Clark

HAZLETON PUBLISHING

PUBLISHER
Richard Poulter

EXECUTIVE PUBLISHER
Elizabeth Le Breton

ART EDITOR
Steve Small

PRODUCTION MANAGER
George Greenfield

HOUSE EDITOR
Peter Lovering

PRODUCTION ASSISTANT
Deirdre Fenney

STATISTICS
John Taylor and Jocelyne Bia

The photograph on the front cover is by Paul-Henri Cahier. The portrait on the back cover is by Diana Burnett.

Black and white photography by:
Autosport Photographic, Jeff Bloxham, Diana Burnett, Colorsport, International Press Agency, Charles Briscoe-Knight and Nigel Snowdon.

Colour photography by:
Autosport Photographic – page 65.
Diana Burnett – pages 72 *(bottom)* and 74.
Lukas Gorys – page 77 *(bottom)*.
Charles Briscoe-Knight – pages 66, 67, 68, 69, 70-1 and 77 *(top)*.
Nigel Snowdon – pages 72 *(top)*, 73, 75, 76, 78-9 and 80.

This first edition published in 1991 by
Hazleton Publishing, 3 Richmond Hill, Richmond,
Surrey TW10 6RE.

ISBN: 0-905138-92-9

Printed in England by BAS Printers Ltd, Over Wallop, Hampshire.

Typesetting by First impression Ltd, Richmond, Surrey.

DISTRIBUTORS

UK & OTHER MARKETS
George Philip Ltd, 59 Grosvenor Street
London W1X 9DA

USA & CANADA
Motorbooks International, PO Box 2
729 Prospect Avenue, Osceola
Wisconsin 54020, USA

AUSTRALIA
Technical Book & Magazine Co. Pty
289-299 Swanston Street
Melbourne, Victoria 3000

Universal Motor Publications
c/o Automoto Motoring Bookshop
152-154 Clarence Street
Sydney 2000, New South Wales

NEW ZEALAND
David Bateman Ltd, 'Golden Heights'
32-34 View Road, Glenfield, Auckland 10

The author would like to thank Motor Racing Publications for permission to quote from Doug Nye's *Theme Lotus*.

PROLOGUE

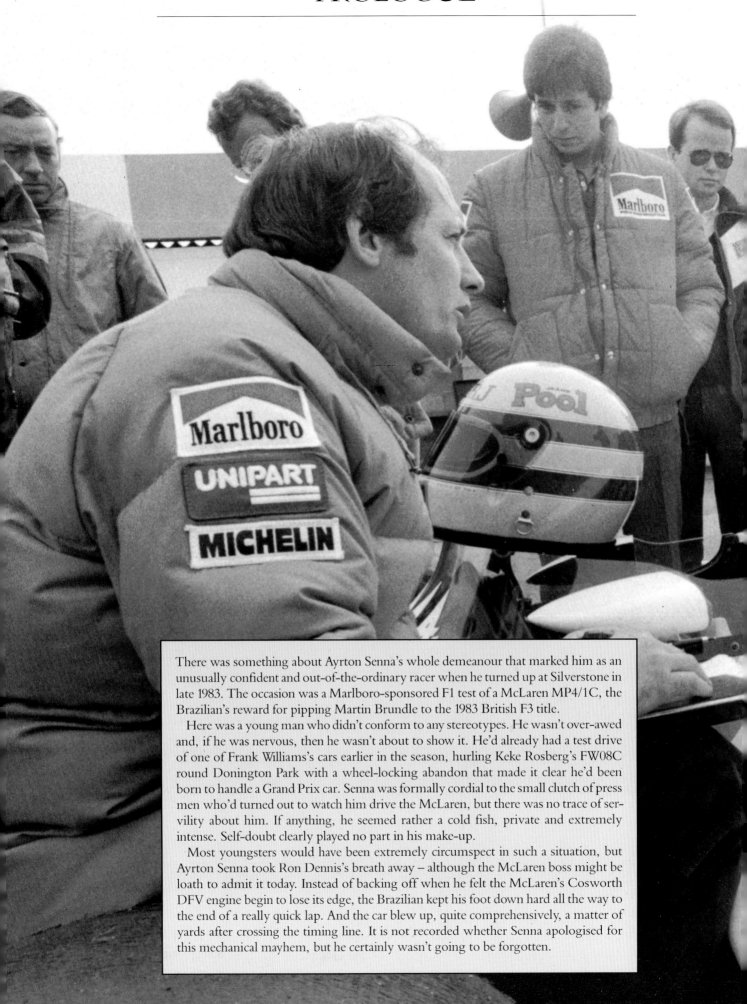

There was something about Ayrton Senna's whole demeanour that marked him as an unusually confident and out-of-the-ordinary racer when he turned up at Silverstone in late 1983. The occasion was a Marlboro-sponsored F1 test of a McLaren MP4/1C, the Brazilian's reward for pipping Martin Brundle to the 1983 British F3 title.

Here was a young man who didn't conform to any stereotypes. He wasn't over-awed and, if he was nervous, then he wasn't about to show it. He'd already had a test drive of one of Frank Williams's cars earlier in the season, hurling Keke Rosberg's FW08C round Donington Park with a wheel-locking abandon that made it clear he'd been born to handle a Grand Prix car. Senna was formally cordial to the small clutch of press men who'd turned out to watch him drive the McLaren, but there was no trace of servility about him. If anything, he seemed rather a cold fish, private and extremely intense. Self-doubt clearly played no part in his make-up.

Most youngsters would have been extremely circumspect in such a situation, but Ayrton Senna took Ron Dennis's breath away – although the McLaren boss might be loath to admit it today. Instead of backing off when he felt the McLaren's Cosworth DFV engine begin to lose its edge, the Brazilian kept his foot down hard all the way to the end of a really quick lap. And the car blew up, quite comprehensively, a matter of yards after crossing the timing line. It is not recorded whether Senna apologised for this mechanical mayhem, but he certainly wasn't going to be forgotten.

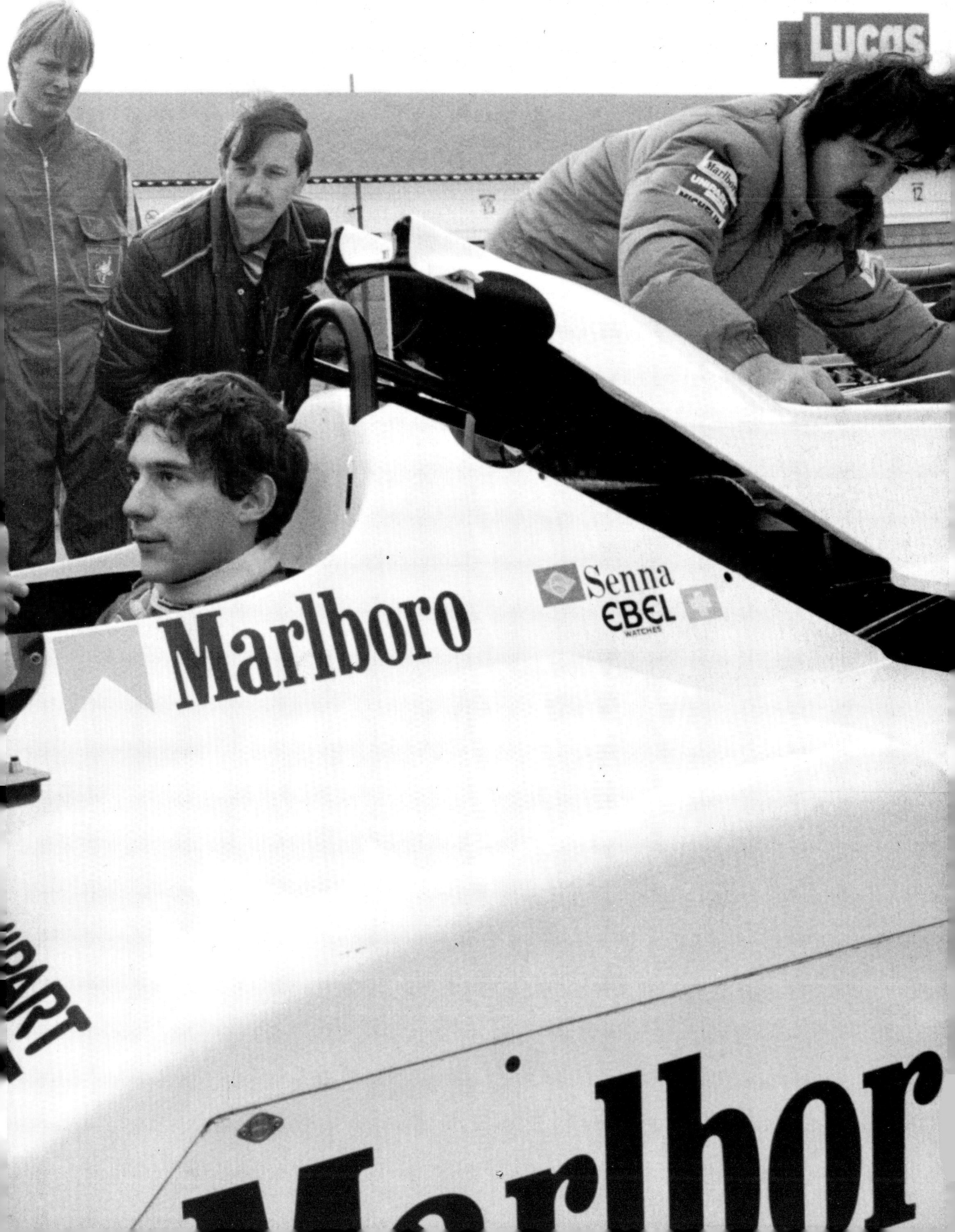
Lucas
Marlboro
Senna
EBEL
WATCHES

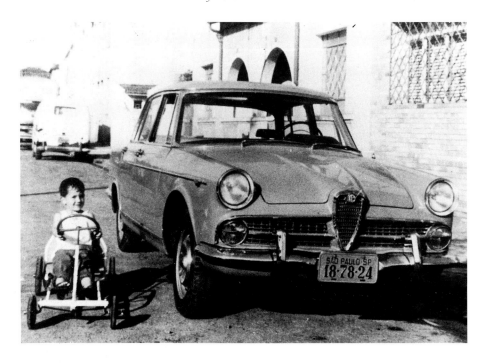

Below: *Ayrton at four years old, on his first home-brewed kart; alongside is the family Alfa Romeo, quite a car for São Paulo in 1964.*

Born on 21 March 1960, the son of wealthy São Paulo businessman Milton da Silva, Ayrton grew up in a secure and comfortable family environment. To this day, he values and fiercely protects the privacy and sense of belonging his upbringing imbued in him. He adores both his family and his native Brazil, speaking of them with respectful affection. To say he was born with a silver spoon in his mouth may be going too far: his father certainly had the wherewithal to insulate him from life's harsher realities, so in that respect he was fortunate, and seems to appreciate it, but he was clearly disciplined well as a child.

Karting provided him with his basic grounding in motor sport. In fact, his father built him a kart when he was only four years old. Later, da Silva Senior disciplined his son with the sanction that if his monthly school reports fell short of the mark, there was no karting for a month. It must have been a painful penalty for the schoolboy enthusiast.

With pedal jeep, already displaying that calm and serious demeanour as a toddler!

Opposite: *A proud Milton da Silva with his elder son.*

Early days: Ayrton competing in kart racing in his native Brazil.

When Ayrton Senna da Silva exploded onto the British national Formula Ford scene
in 1981, most observers simply saw yet another unusually talented Brazilian following
in the footsteps of several celebrated countrymen. But, as is often the case, there was
a lot more hard racing experience underpinning his efforts than one might have suspected.
By then he had been kart racing for eight years, having made his debut in July 1973.

Starting in the 100 cc category, where he remained for his first few years of racing,
he then decided to have a crack at the World Championship. Held at Le Mans in 1977,
and at Estoril two years later, young Senna da Silva contested both of these one-race
shoot-outs. He managed sixth in the former event and finished runner-up to Dutch-
man Peter Koene in 1979 having been defeated, in effect, by the complexities of the
aggregate scoring system which placed a premium on the best two results out of the
three finals. He was second again in 1980, the championship contested this time at Bel-
gium's Nivelles circuit. The following season he was up and running in Formula Ford.

For 1981 he beat a path to Ralph Firman's door and fixed himself up with a Van
Diemen FF1600 machine. Firman recalls him as being unusually determined, but John
Kirkpatrick, long-time manager of the Jim Russell Racing Drivers' School – now at
Donington Park, but then at Snetterton – remembers him as a very quiet and totally
unobtrusive youngster. 'If a group of us went down to the pub, he would come along,
but he would just stand quietly to one side, sipping his drink, and only seemed to speak
when spoken to. He was really very shy.'

Ayrton won his third race, setting the tone for the year. By the end of the season he
had taken the chequered flag 12 times in 20 races, clinching both the RAC and
Townsend Thoresen titles. But the Brazilian finished the year in a somewhat confused
state of mind, disillusioned that advancement even from this lowly level depended
every bit as much on the financial resources available as on sheer talent. It was a conun-
drum which he couldn't fully understand – and it annoyed him. Moreover, life in rural
Norfolk had taken its toll on his marriage to Liliane, his childhood sweetheart. He
returned to Brazil that winter and almost turned his back on motor racing for good.
There was talk of his going into the family business, learning about cattle in order to
help his father manage their huge Brazilian ranch in Goiânia. Eventually, however, he
came to terms with the vagaries of racing, raised the finance and returned to England
for the 1982 season. Alone. 'I just couldn't resist the attraction of a steering wheel and
a racing car,' he reflected in 1988. 'Up to that point I had raced largely for fun and, if I
had not come back to England, I would probably have continued racing, just as a
hobby, in Brazil.'

He had hoped to graduate to F3 but the budget was not available, so he opted to run a semi-works Van Diemen in Formula Ford 2000, entered by Rushen Green Racing. His blitz on both the British and European series made his FF1600 exploits pale into absolute insignificance. This time he won 21 out of the 27 races in which he took part, including triumphs in front of the F1 fraternity at Zolder, Hockenheim and the Öster-reichring. People were undoubtedly impressed, but there was definitely an underlying feeling that FF2000 couldn't be exactly the most competitive of arenas if this young Brazilian could produce this level of domination. Wait until he gets to F3, said the doubters, then it will be different.

It wasn't. At the end of the year he arranged a drive in a West Surrey Racing Ralt at the televised Thruxton meeting. Starting from pole, he won handsomely. To some extent the outing could be regarded as an opportunity for some mutual assessment between the two parties, prior to finalising a deal for a full-scale assault on the British F3 Championship the following year.

Opposite: *Ayrton's 1983 British F3 Championship campaign was highlighted by his close battle for the title with Martin Brundle. Senna's mount was a Ralt RT3 prepared by West Surrey Racing* (below), *which he also took to a prestigious victory in the Macau GP* (below left).

That series polarised into a battle between Ayrton (who for racing purposes had dropped his paternal family surname, preferring to be known simply by his mother's family name, Senna – just as Nelson Piquet Sauto-Maior had done some years earlier) and British rising star Martin Brundle. In a season punctuated by several spectacular shunts, a by-product of Ayrton's absolute refusal to accept second best, the Brazilian pipped his English rival at the very last race, and took the British title. Finally, to round off the year, he won superbly at Macau. Unsurprisingly, Ayrton remains unshakeably convinced of the value of F3 as an international training ground. He firmly rejects the notion that this junior category is hamstrung by lack of power and too much grip. 'No, no . . . it teaches you discipline, experience, how to behave from a technical point of view. It teaches you how to drive with economy of effort.'

But there was much more to Ayrton Senna than simply an ability to win motor races. As Frank Williams, who presided over that maiden F1 test at Donington, was quick to realise, this Brazilian was unusually intelligent and articulate. He could describe how the car was behaving in lucid, graphic detail. It was the continuation of a trait first noticed by Dennis Rushen and Robin Green in Ayrton's FF2000 Van Diemen days. Senna had a rare gift: the capacity to slow the whole car performance process down in his mind – and this ability was linked to an uncanny sensitivity when it came to assessing how quickly it might be possible to lap. Only occasionally would his Latin temperament bubble through to the surface and cause him to do something slightly unpredictable.

By the time Senna was winning at Macau in Bennetts's F3 Ralt, the die had been cast for his F1 career. Already there were people queuing up for the services of this remarkably committed new boy. Bernie Ecclestone was keen to have him alongside Nelson Piquet at Brabham and, indeed, at the 1983 British Grand Prix the elder Brazilian spent a long time chatting to the new star. Senna was later to say that Piquet had indicated he would not object if he joined the team. However, much as Bernie wanted that to happen, constraints imposed by various sponsorship agreements blocked it. 'I don't know whether Nelson also eventually said no,' Ayrton later reflected, 'but if he did, I can't say I would have blamed him . . .'

Eventually Ayrton decided to go to Toleman – ironically, as it turned out later, as successor to the Renault-bound Derek Warwick – but not before Peter Warr had tried energetically to recruit the Brazilian rising star into the Team Lotus fold. However, Imperial Tobacco had been keen to retain Nigel Mansell and Senna, showing shrewd judgement, preferred to make his Grand Prix debut with a less celebrated team, keeping the pressure on himself to a minimum as he learnt the ropes. It was not a process that would take him very long.

Toleman team-chief Alex Hawkridge quickly realised the long-term quality of their new recruit. He was also impressed, and sometimes a little indignant, with Ayrton's forthright approach. 'No matter what the situation, he always, without exception, felt that he was right,' reflected Hawkridge, 'and what made it even more infuriating at times was that he was generally correct. His capacity to control and channel his emotions was also remarkable. But he could be two distinct personalities. Watching the painstaking manner in which he scrutinised his contract with us, that meticulous attention to detail, contrasted with his off-duty character – socially, he could become schoolboyish, almost giggly.'

Yet, even at this early stage of his career, one was aware that the unduly intelligent Brazilian was someone special. Over the next four seasons he was to develop into a man so totally absorbed by every detail of his work – his obsession – that only a few people, working alongside him, with his team, can make contact with him. He radiates such an all-pervading feeling of intense concentration that one gets the impression he is attempting to probe every inner technical facet of his car's make-up. This sort of approach leaves no room for the frivolous. Talking to Senna involves shifting up a gear mentally. Small talk isn't to his taste, but ask a very specific and detailed question and he will respond in correspondingly painstaking vein. He doesn't deal in 'ifs' and 'maybes'.

None of his answers is superficial, and although English is a foreign language to him, the way in which he has mastered it stands as an acute embarrassment to those of us who, at best, can only mumble the odd few phrases in tourist French. Talking to him prior to the 1988 Portuguese Grand Prix, we touched on the subject of a test session he had carried out with the new Honda V10-engined prototype at the tiny Pembrey track in South Wales. 'Down the M4, just beyond Port Talbot, isn't it?' I enquired. 'Near *Llanelli*, actually,' he explained. It stopped me in my tracks. Richard Burton couldn't have pronounced 'Llanelli' more accurately . . .

Senna's talent was such that it quickly outgrew what Toleman could offer him. The team began 1984 with the Hart-engined TG183B and Ayrton scored his first World Championship point at Kyalami, the second race on the calendar. But it was clear that Pirelli's rubber was simply not on the same competitive level as the contemporary Michelins, so after a truncated and unsatisfactory weekend at Imola, which saw Senna failing to qualify for the San Marino Grand Prix, a switch to the French rubber was engineered in time for the French Grand Prix at Dijon-Prenois. Both Ayrton and team-mate Johnny Cecotto retired their brand new TG184s with turbo failure – but next on the race calendar was Monaco, where Senna was destined to put his name up in lights.

Ayrton qualified 13th and lined up with his colleagues on a rain-soaked starting grid for one of the wettest races in Monaco history. Splashing through the murk, he steadily picked up the pace and began to work his way through the pack, looking for all the world as though he had been driving F1 cars in such dire conditions all his life.

Pre-Canadian Grand Prix football match, 1984;
Ayrton (front row, extreme right) *is alongside*
Derek Warwick.

By lap 16 he was up to third, and had Niki Lauda's McLaren firmly in his sights. It only took him another three laps to overtake the Austrian twice World Champion, after which he set off purposefully after Prost. Coming up to the 30-lap mark the rain intensified; Ayrton had moved to within seven seconds of the McLaren, surviving a hair-raising incident when he glanced the chicance kerb, briefly two-wheeling his TG184, but retaining control. By now Prost was signalling skywards that Clerk of the Course Jacky Ickx should stop the race as the track was virtually flooded.

On lap 33, Ickx obliged and Prost pulled over to the right as he saw the chequered flag, allowing Senna to burst past on a cloud of spume and cross the line first. Ayrton thought he had won! He later felt cheated – as did the rest of the Toleman team – when everybody realised that in such circumstances the race order is taken on the lap *prior* to the chequered flag. Half points were awarded for this event – but Senna had made his mark.

Wet-weather form has always been one of the crucial indices by which one judges great racing drivers and Ayrton Senna certainly stands up to scrutiny in this respect. In fact, when one analyses his career performance over the years, wet-weather brilliance has been one of the crucial cornerstones of his success. In 1985, he was to win his first Grand Prix, in a Lotus 97T-Renault at Estoril, in conditions so appalling that Alain Prost's McLaren spun out of the race on the start/finish straight. Three years later this same skill would win him the British Grand Prix at Silverstone and the German Grand Prix at Hockenheim, both giant strides towards his World Championship title. Bearing this capability in mind, there was something peculiarly ironic about the way in which Senna drove the last few laps of the race which clinched his first World Championship, the 1988 Japanese Grand Prix, pointing anxiously skywards to indicate to race officials (in an ironic echo of Prost at Monaco in 1984) that another light shower was brushing Suzuka and that perhaps they ought to think about flagging the race early. But then, of course, they were all on slicks on this occasion . . .

Throughout the summer of 1984 Senna consolidated his reputation. Third place at Brands Hatch behind Lauda's McLaren and Warwick's Renault proved to be another significant feather in his cap, and there were already rumblings of interest in his services from other teams, notably Lotus. Peter Warr was extremely anxious to secure the services of the man he was later to describe as 'in my experience the most complete driver since Jimmy Clark'. He convinced his sponsors that Senna was the man and duly signed him just prior to the 1984 Dutch Grand Prix.

Much has been written on the subject of Senna's departure from Toleman. He did, indeed, have a buy-out clause which was duly exercised, but Alex Hawkridge contends

The victory rostrum for the 1984 British Grand Prix.
Senna (right) *has just brought his Toleman home third,*
behind Niki Lauda's winning McLaren and the
Renault of Derek Warwick.

*Early laps at Detroit, '84. Senna's Toleman leads Martin
Brundle's Tyrrell, Thierry Boutsen's Arrows, the Ferrari
of René Arnoux, Stefan Bellof's Tyrrell and Ayrton's
Toleman team-mate, Johnny Cecotto.*

Below: *In conversation with Toleman team-manager
Peter Gethin, one of the few people who seemed to have
something of a calming influence on the young
Brazilian in '84.*

to this day that Ayrton handled the whole situation with a lack of delicacy. Although
Peter Warr might have thought this was nonsense at the time, those who saw the
Lotus team-manager's face in 1987, when it became clear that Ayrton was not staying
on for a fourth year, would have concluded that 'what goes around, comes around'.
Yet Senna remains enigmatic on the subject and one is left with the strong impression
that he wants to brush the precise details of his departure from Toleman under the car-
pet. To him it's just history, a detail from the past, buried in the deeper recesses of his
mind.

Hawkridge really got the Brazilian's attention when he suspended him from the Italian Grand Prix at Monza – Stefan Johansson stood in for him and finished fourth – but
he was back behind the wheel of the TG184 for the European Grand Prix at the new
Nürburgring. He became embroiled in a multiple shunt at the first corner there, but
rounded off the year in glorious style when his Toleman-Hart swept home imperiously
at Estoril, third only to the McLaren-TAGs of Prost and new World Champion Lauda.

*Chaos in the European Grand Prix at the Nürburgring.
The pack scatters after Senna's Toleman (19) has
collided with Rosberg's Williams. Also autocrossing in
this shot are Ghinzani's Osella, Laffite's Williams,
Mansell's Lotus and Surer's Arrows.*

Ayrton heads the Toleman TG184 to a magnificent third
place in the Portuguese Grand Prix at Estoril to round
off his association with the team.

Even in 1988, when I suggested to him that, legal wrangling aside, he had left Toleman because their technical capabilities fell short of his own personal aspirations, he
rejected the contention – albeit enigmatically. 'That's not correct,' he replied. 'I don't
know whether it's worth going back that much, I'm not really interested. Just say that
I actually left Toleman not because of technical things, but because of other reasons. I
was actually very happy to stay and carry on my career with the people there. I thought
they were competent and good to give me the opportunity to learn. So that was not
the reason.'

In the next breath he explained his move to Lotus as 'the right direction' at the time,
so one is bound to consider other factors when attempting to analyse why he exercised
his release option. Looking back, when Toleman split with Pirelli and changed to
Michelin, the Italian tyre company's door slammed very firmly behind them. Then,
at the end of 1984, Michelin withdrew and Goodyear, overburdened with existing
commitments, in addition to taking on former prestige Michelin runners like McLaren
and Renault, just didn't have the capacity to supply Toleman as well. Hawkridge was
advised in good time by Akron that this would be the case, so perhaps Senna read the
way the situation was developing well in advance and opted for a move. In any case,
the Lotus-Renault package had looked consistently promising in the hands of Elio de
Angelis and Nigel Mansell over the previous couple of seasons – and, up to that point,
neither of those drivers was perceived to be in the same class as Senna.

Keeping his Lotus 97T ahead of Alain Prost's
McLaren during the 1985 San Marino GP.
Ayrton ran out of fuel, Prost was disqualified
and Elio de Angelis won!

Peter Warr told author Doug Nye in his book *Theme Lotus*: 'Colin Chapman used to say that in any one year there are three, possibly four drivers in the running for the World Championship who always had to be regarded as natural Grand Prix winners. Our drivers, when I returned to Lotus in 1982, didn't figure in that élite group. In effect, we had two number twos and it stayed that way until 1985 when we took on Ayrton Senna. His class was so obvious that, when he joined us that season, I had offered him number one status, with Elio to decide if he wanted to stay, but Ayrton turned it down, preferring to be joint number one in what was still only his second season of F1 racing, so that he could learn the trade . . . but he soon made it clear that he was the number one out on the track.'

It was typical of Senna's analytical off-circuit approach that he wanted to handle his first season in a front-line team as shrewdly as possible, turning the situation to his best advantage. He was quicker than de Angelis from the outset, yet ironically Elio opened the year with a third place at Rio, where Ayrton retired. Then came Estoril – in the pouring rain. Senna, the newcomer, scarcely put a wheel out of line to win brilliantly in streaming wet conditions. He was on the verge of unlocking that enormous potential.

His first season at Lotus was not without its problems, however. Alain Prost criticised him roundly for what the Frenchman regarded as his blocking tactics at Imola, where the two of them battled long and hard for the lead of the San Marino Grand Prix. Prost was eventually first past the flag, after Senna ran out of fuel, but the McLaren-TAG was subsequently found to be slightly underweight at post-race scrutineering.

Ayrton is greeted by team-manager Peter Warr and the
rest of the Lotus crew after scoring the marque's first
victory in almost three years.

It was disqualified, handing victory to none other than de Angelis in the other Lotus. Later Senna would also lead the British Grand Prix commandingly, only for his 97T to run out of fuel again, allowing Prost through to an unchallenged win. These performances gave rise to speculation that Ayrton had simply been winding up the boost pressure in a desperate bid to lead the two races. On closer examination, that contention short-changed the Brazilian's common sense. At Imola his Lotus had been fitted with the less fuel-efficient Renault EF4 engine rather than the newer EF15 (which was installed in his team-mate's car), while at Silverstone a broken sensor in the electronic management system caused one bank of cylinders to lurch onto full-rich, destroying his carefully planned consumption calculations.

Senna recalls Silverstone as one of his most satisfying races, even though it didn't produce a firm result. 'If you have a good car, then you enjoy yourself,' he later reflected. 'At Silverstone in 1985 my Lotus was running really well. OK, it failed to finish, but I came away satisfied because I had been running strong and fast, in complete control of what I was doing.' He contrasted that outing with his third-place finish at Monaco the following year, behind the McLaren-TAGs of Prost and Keke Rosberg: 'Sure, I was on the podium in third place, behind the two McLarens, but the car was a disaster to drive and it was a tremendously hard race. I did not feel particularly happy about it.'

There were other disappointments in 1985, notably suffering an engine failure at Monaco after qualifying superbly on pole. He had momentarily over-revved the engine, during the race morning warm-up; the team, already working flat-out to change the Renault V6 in Elio's 97T, asked him if he would race it anyway. He did so, but he was sufficiently shrewd to realise that he had done damage to the engine that was potentially terminal – and so it proved.

None the less, Senna's second Grand Prix win was to come at Spa that year, where he headed Nigel Mansell's Williams FW10 home. He then took second billing to the Englishman in the Grand Prix of Europe at Brands Hatch and failed to finish at both Kyalami and Adelaide. The latter race, in fact, produced an untypically erratic performance by Lotus's new star, which not only encompassed a couple of wild excursions off the circuit, but also saw him wiping off the fins of his nose against the back of Rosberg's winning Williams. Eventually the 97T's Renault engine spewed most of a piston into its inlet tract and Ayrton's most inconsistent F1 race was over. To this day, nobody has ever been quite sure why Senna was so wild and unrestrained on that particular occasion, although it has been suggested that a slight ear infection, resulting from a water-skiing accident while he was on holiday in Mauritius, might have upset his finely honed sense of balance. Ayrton ended up fourth in the 1985 World Championship, on 38 points; Prost won the title with 73 points.

Senna's first season at Lotus had been moderately successful, but nowhere near as productive as he would have liked. It had, however, helped him to reach two conclusions. First, he now wanted to take over the mantle of undisputed number one driver for 1986. Second, since Team Lotus was demonstrably incapable of producing two reliably competitive cars to the same technical standard, he did not want a number two who was going to deflect the team's resources from his own efforts. This single-mindedness was to lead to a major controversy over the question of Derek Warwick's inclusion in the team.

The Englishman was facing F1 unemployment, now that Renault was withdrawing its factory team from F1, and Peter Warr was anxious to include him in the Lotus line-up. Warr remained convinced that Warwick would dutifully play second fiddle to Senna, but Ayrton was not so sure, contract or no contract. Inwardly, he felt that Derek would not really be happy fulfilling a supporting role, and foregoing access to the spare car, after having a sniff of success with Renault.

Warr spent a long time trying to argue Senna out of his position, to the accompaniment of critical voices from the British press (including the author's) who felt that the Lotus team-manager was allowing his authority to be undermined by his number one driver. Senna, having already had a rough ride from the English media over the manner of his departure from Toleman, wasn't at all amused by the fuss. Indeed, there is still evidence that the rift between him and the fourth estate has never fully healed.

Eventually, Lotus settled on a compromise candidate, F3 graduate Johnny Dumfries. The aristocratic Scot was destined to do an unobtrusive and workmanlike job in the

37

second car, never giving Ayrton a moment's worry. On reflection, one can state unequivocally that Ayrton had absolutely nothing at all against Warwick personally; his concern was basically about Lotus's engineering shortcomings.

For 1986 Gérard Ducarouge penned the new Lotus 98T which, powered by the latest, greatly modified version of the Renault EF15 V6, was now equipped with a highly promising pneumatic valve-closing system. This allowed the engine speed to be increased from 11,000 to 12,500 rpm. Thus armed, Senna qualified nine times in pole position, yet he added only two more Grand Prix victories to his tally. One success was through the streets of Detroit, where his delicate touch and precise throttle control reaped benefits; the other was a split-second win over Nigel Mansell's Williams-Honda at Jerez in the Spanish Grand Prix. It didn't take a clairvoyant to see that a Honda engine was needed if a driver was to run consistently at the front of the Grand Prix field.

By now Senna was sharing a large house in the Esher stockbroker belt with his old pal Mauricio Gugelmin and his wife Stella. It was a comfortably relaxed and familiar environment for the young man, who still didn't really enjoy being away from his family and friends in Brazil. The talk was of motor racing, techniques and deals, Ayrton spending long evenings analysing page after page of the Longines individual lap-time print-outs from the various races, and only allowing himself a break from matters motor racing to fly his scale model aeroplanes, his fast-mushrooming off-track preoccupation.

'I first got involved with them through a friend in 1985, at around the time of the Brands Hatch Grand Prix,' he explains, 'and I've got more and more involved ever since. They have 10 or 20 cc engines, running on special fuel and, yes, while there are competitions in which you can take part, I just fly them for pure pleasure.' Those who have seen him putting his planes through their paces will testify to a level of daring and commitment matched only by his exploits behind the wheel of a Grand Prix car . . .

The 1986 season developed into a three-way battle for the championship between Nelson Piquet, Nigel Mansell and McLaren's Alain Prost, the Frenchman slipping through to grab his second successive title from the warring Williams-Honda teamsters at the very last race of the year. The Frenchman finished the season on 70 points, Senna trailing in fourth once more with 55 points. By the end of the season Ayrton Senna had reached something of a turning-point. Three years into his F1 career there was no doubt that a mere four Grand Prix victories were scarcely an accurate representation of either his ability level or his potential. But, as he would remark frequently, 'Every time I go out and race, I am there only because I believe it is possible to win.'

Ayrton completes the first lap of the 1986 Detroit Grand
Prix ahead of the Williams of Nigel Mansell and René
Arnoux's Ligier. He went on to score his second victory
of the season.

Images of '86. Clockwise: Sharing the rostrum with Nelson Piquet after finishing second at Rio; a moment's relaxation; contemplating his practice times at Jerez; with two-wheeled transportation at Monza; chasing the McLarens at Monaco.

Mansell and Piquet had proved that, all else being equal, a Honda turbo was fast becoming a necessary prerequisite for any sustained success. Lotus therefore finalised a deal to acquire Honda engines in 1987, at least partly in exchange for agreeing to take Japanese journeyman Satoru Nakajima as Senna's team-mate. Moreover, Lotus had a trick or two up their sleeve in the form of the computer-controlled active suspension system which, it was hoped, would give the new 99T a winning edge over the Williams-Hondas. But as early as the eve of his 1987 Monaco victory, Senna had not only assessed the car's potential *vis-à-vis* the Williams FW11Bs, but was also almost certainly on the verge of concluding a deal to move to McLaren in 1988.

With the benefit of hindsight, the remarks made by Senna in an interview I taped with him at Monaco are even more illuminating and significant than they seemed at the time. In response to my asking him whether he considered this year (1987) as a development season for the active suspension, on which he could build to win the title in 1988, he responded with a firm 'no'. I then asked him whether he felt he could win the 1987 title. A longer pause – followed by another 'no'.

It quickly became clear to Senna that, from an aerodynamic standpoint, the Lotus-Honda wasn't up to the standard of the Williams, while the sheer volume of technical input from the active suspension system simply could not be monitored and analysed quickly enough during the crowded racing calendar. He was to win at Monaco, but only after Mansell's Williams retired, and while the benefits of the active suspension system made life less stressful over the corrugations of Detroit, where he scored his only other victory of the year, in general terms the Lotus could not offer that elusive, winning edge.

Ayrton and the team were undeniably happy that the system had at least been reliable from the outset, but there were clearly other aspects of the 99T's performance that lagged behind the front-line opposition. 'At the start of the active suspension programme we were perhaps a little over-optimistic about the length of time it would take to produce a measurable performance advantage,' Senna explained. 'The season was an enormous challenge for everybody at Lotus, with a new car, new engine, new suspension and new gearbox, so we anticipated many problems. But we decided to race the active system at Rio and, while it was reliable, I felt the car was moving around too much.

'We improved it considerably in time for Imola and, although we faced a major handling imbalance at Spa, by the time we got to qualifying at Monaco I felt it was working very well. The system has enormous potential and each time I drove the car I realised

Ayrton shares the rostrum with Nelson Piquet after his
second successive victory in the Detroit Grand Prix.

how little I really understood about the car's set-up. You see, it provides so much information that you could relate to what you recall in a particular corner, for example, and it provides you with a lot of material that you would not have otherwise appreciated.

'However, the system is so complex that there is always scope for improvement, even when it is working well. If we were using the conventional passive suspension, then I think we might have discovered that our other problems with the car would actually have been greater.'

This promise notwithstanding, Senna had decided on a change of team before Hockenheim and, in the week following the German race, his lawyers wrote to Team Lotus informing them of Ayrton's intention to move on for 1988. It wasn't until Monza that the F1 fraternity received official word that he would be driving a Marlboro McLaren-Honda alongside Alain Prost in 1988.

From time to time, throughout his career, even Ayrton's most ardent fans would have to concede there could occasionally be a hint of desperation about his driving, usually when things were not going his way. In 1987, as he wrestled to keep his championship hopes alive with the recalcitrant Lotus-Honda, that desperation surfaced several times.

At Hockenheim Senna attracted the wrath of Michele Alboreto – he had nearly put the Ferrari driver off the circuit by weaving on the straight – and the Italian was almost grey with indignation. (It had been the same back in '85, when Ayrton, having taken pole at Monaco, cruised round slowly on the racing line, apparently intent on spoiling the chances of his rivals Alboreto and Niki Lauda. This was one of the very few occasions in his career that I actually saw Lauda lose his temper.) 'With his talent, he just doesn't have to do that,' Alboreto complained, although it has to be said that Michele is hardly an innocent when it comes to adopting awkward racing lines. But Senna did just that at Hockenheim, surviving to finish second despite his Lotus 'collapsing' onto its 'reserve' springs after the active suspension sprang a leak and lost all its hydraulic fluid. It was a real never-say-die, dogged performance by the Brazilian: he just didn't know how to give up.

Alboreto settled the score at the Österreichring, brake-testing Senna to send him scuttling for a replacement nose cone, but at Monza his heroic gamble on a non-stop run almost paid off. With seven laps to go he was hanging on just ahead of Piquet's Williams when he slid onto the dirt at the Parabolica, allowing the other Brazilian through to victory. Ayrton recovered to finish second, only 1.8s down. He tried for a non-stop run at Jerez, as well, holding up a great queue of faster cars, before fading to fifth. It was a performance which seemed a bit extreme, to say the least, even attracting admonishing remarks from former World Champion Jackie Stewart.

Ayrton keeps the Lotus-Honda ahead of the Ferraris of
Michele Alboreto and Gerhard Berger during the 1987
Spanish GP at Jerez where he finished fifth after
encountering tyre problems.

Opposite: *Grand alliance. Prost and Senna with the
MP4/4-Honda at Rio, prior to the '88 Brazilian
Grand Prix.*

*Unlocking the key to '88. Ayrton in company with
Alain Prost, Ron Dennis and Honda's Yoshitoshi
Sakurai at the McLaren-Honda announcement,
Monza 1987.*

Probably the most memorable episode of that action-packed 1987 season came at Spa, where Nigel Mansell took him off on the opening lap and, the Englishman having decided that the incident was Senna's fault, later attempted to thump him when they squared up to each other in the Team Lotus pit garage. Ayrton also shunted hard during practice at Mexico City, where his title chances finally evaporated, and he rounded off his Lotus career by being disqualified from second place in Adelaide, where the 99T's extra front brake cooling ducts were deemed to infringe the permissible coachwork dimensions.

For 1988, he faced the prospect of battling with Alain Prost, a rival he admitted he respected 'not only for his driving, but for his whole manner, his achievement, his behaviour'. He was also striding into Prost's personal enclave, where the Frenchman was popularly established. Many people felt that Ayrton would have the upper hand from race to race, but that the canny Prost would have the overall edge, taken throughout the championship campaign.

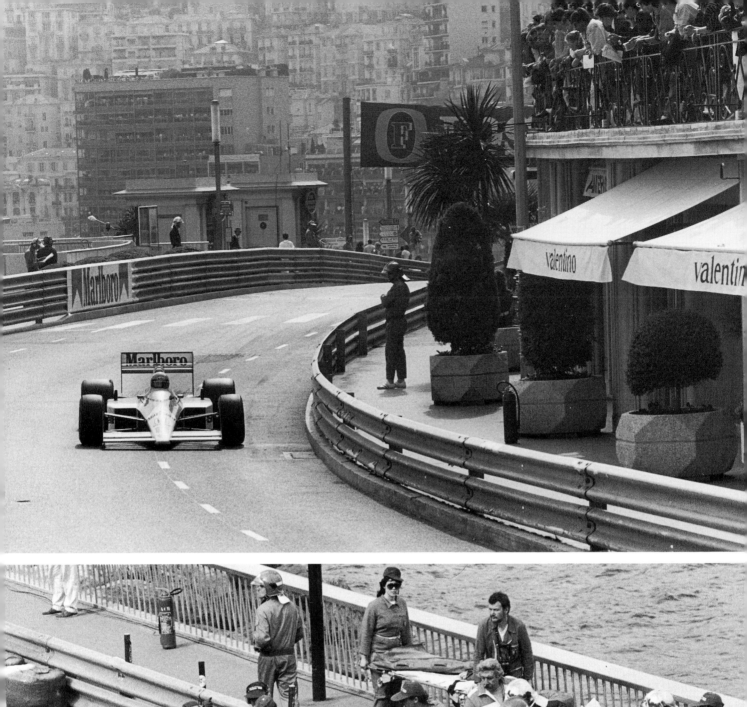

Sure enough, Prost kicked off with a win at Rio, the new MP4/4-Honda turbo demonstrating a level of technical superiority such as to make the World Championship contest the McLaren team's personal property. Psychology played a major part in the relationship between these two outstandingly talented drivers who, while sharing the same competitive urges, are as different as chalk from cheese. On the one hand, Prost: gregarious, easy-going, imbued with a wicked sense of humour and with a relaxed manner thinly concealing his professionalism and commitment. On the other, Senna: obsessive, intense, almost dour, and totally absorbed in the technocratic challenge of making a Grand Prix car operate to its absolute optimum.

Ayrton qualified on pole at Rio, but gearchange problems spiked his challenge even before the start. He was eventually black-flagged and disqualified for changing to the spare car after the green flag had been waved to indicate the start of the pre-race parade lap. So Prost finished the day nine points ahead.

At Imola Ayrton was on pole again and now showed what he could do. He led from start to finish, contending with a slight gear-linkage gremlin which almost pitched him into a spin at one point. But Prost came back to win at Monaco after Ayrton, the race apparently in the bag, slid into the wall at the Portier right-hander, removing his McLaren's left-front wheel.

'I'd driven almost the perfect race,' he reflects, 'probably the best I'd ever done in terms of qualifying, race performance and car set-up – until the end. There were some reasons behind it, of which I was aware, but to which I wasn't reacting. Earlier, I had a moment in Casino Square when the car jumped out of gear as I began to relax. I nearly hit the barrier. I got myself back into a rhythm, but then the same process happened again and this time it caught me out.'

Later, after clinching the World Championship at Suzuka, Ayrton conceded that Monaco was the turning-point of the year. He considered that, psychologically, he changed a lot after that mistake woke him up: 'I have to say it also brought me closer to God than I had ever been, and has changed my life completely . . .'

In terms of accepted professionalism, however, his decision to return immediately to his nearby flat – his European base when away from his beloved Brazil – amounted to a major breach of team etiquette. For over three hours Ron Dennis had no first-hand information as to what had caused the shunt. The team were not amused, although Senna later professed not to know what on earth all the fuss was about. His supporters would argue that this intensely egocentric streak helps make him the driver he unquestionably is. The fact remains, though, that the team were extremely disappointed with his behaviour on that particular occasion.

. . . until he hit that wall. Derek Warwick, passing,
must have suppressed a smile.

Below: *Shaving the walls in Downtown Motown,
heading for his Detroit Grand Prix hat-trick.*

They were not often disappointed, of course. Prost, meanwhile, inherited victory at Monaco and went on to beat Ayrton in Mexico, the Brazilian hampered by a faulty pop-off valve and higher-than-expected fuel consumption. Four races down, and Prost had won three of them.

Alain was relieved, but knew pretty well what to expect in Montreal and Detroit, where Senna's audacity in traffic was certain to pay dividends. The Frenchman led initially in Canada, only to be muscled aside and then dropped as Ayrton shimmered through gaps that hardly looked as though they were there. Alain had been around for too long to be interested in heroics of that sort. He was second in both races.

Gearchange problems intervened again at Paul Ricard, where Ayrton was not only beaten to pole position by Prost, but headed across the line at the end of a race which had seen the Frenchman snatch the lead in a brilliantly opportunist manoeuvre, as the two McLarens threaded their path through the back-markers.

A study in concentration at Monaco with the MP4/4.

Senna had been trailing Prost in the championship points table ever since Rio, but the next couple of races would see his title aspirations rise dramatically. Moreover, there was to be a certain irony in the way the pattern of the season developed for Prost. Never one to conceal his dislike of racing in the rain, the Frenchman was dealt a most unfortunate hand at both Silverstone and Hockenheim when the British and German Grands Prix became the first wet races for three years – since Ayrton Senna won at Estoril for Lotus, in fact!

At Silverstone, major aerodynamic revisions to the turbo ducting within the MP4/4 side pods somewhat scrambled the team's technical progress throughout qualifying, leaving Senna and Prost on the second row of the grid behind the Ferraris of Gerhard Berger and Michele Alboreto. During qualifying Ayrton's remarkable qualities of icy cool were put on public display when he twice pirouetted the McLaren-Honda exiting Stowe Corner. Before the tyre smoke had cleared, he engaged a lower gear and accelerated away from the incident, the McLaren having never come to a standstill . . .

The race itself was controversial for the McLaren team, although not on Ayrton's part. In streaming rain, he tailed Berger's Ferrari for the first 14 laps before ducking through into the lead, under braking for the Woodcote chicane. The depth of Prost's problems that day can be realised from the fact that Ayrton lapped him as he slipped ahead of Berger. In fact, if it hadn't been for Alain giving him room as he came through under braking, the two MP4/4s might well have collided. Prost simply could not get his car to work in the appalling conditions and he eventually chose to retire after a humiliating midfield performance. Clearly, there was something very badly wrong with his chassis set-up, but he made no apology for his decision to withdraw. Typical Prost, he remained very much his own man.

It was much the same story at Hockenheim. Ayrton ran away into the distance, but this time Alain salvaged his reputation with a strong second, albeit punctuated by a spin over the rain-slicked kerb at the Ostkurve. The Grand Prix action then moved behind the Iron Curtain, to the Hungaroring, where Ayrton battled furiously for pole position with the naturally aspirated Williams FW12 of Nigel Mansell and Thierry Boutsen's Benetton B188. This was one of the few circuits where the non-turbos reckoned they might have a realistic crack at the 2.5-bar/150-litre turbos, but while Mansell tailed Ayrton doggedly in the opening stages, the Englishman was suffering badly from the after-effects of a secondary chicken-pox infection and proved incapable of lasting the distance.

Prost, meanwhile, had qualified a lowly seventh. He spent the early stages of the race

Opposite: *Stripped for action. Senna sits in the McLaren MP4/4 cockpit as mechanics prepare the Honda V6 turbo-engined car for action in the pit lane at Budapest.*

Prost's MP4/4 is almost completely hidden behind Senna's sister-car at the Hungaroring, 1988, and that's where the Frenchman ended up at the chequered flag. Thierry Boutsen watches the action from the cockpit of his Benetton.

conserving as much fuel as he possibly could in the queue behind Senna. Alain rightly figured that his car was quicker than Ayrton's on this particular afternoon, but while keeping pace with the Brazilian might have been one thing, passing him was very definitely a different proposition. He pressed home his attack, though, and eventually managed to ease inside Ayrton, going into the downhill right-hander after the pits, as Senna was busy overtaking Philippe Alliot's Lola and Gabriele Tarquini's Coloni, who were having their own private joust.

Alain came in too quickly, on too tight a line. 'I knew he was quicker than me, so I had to get past him again at the earliest opportunity,' Ayrton explained. Prost immediately handed him back the initiative by sliding wide, away from the apex. Senna ducked round the back of his team-mate and regained the lead before the end of the corner. Prost eased back now, worried by a slight front-wheel vibration which was, in fact, nothing more than debris picked up by his tyres. In the closing moments of the race he spurted back onto Senna's tail, but there was just no way through: the two McLarens sailed past the chequered flag less than a second apart.

Supreme performance. Ayrton runs away with the 1988 Belgian Grand Prix at Spa to make it four successive victories in barely six weeks.

This was a crucial moment for Senna, the day on which he finally drew level with Prost on points. From here he went on to win the Belgian Grand Prix at Spa, destroying Prost's challenge in a straight fight, the Frenchman's ability to respond blunted when he gambled on reducing his MP4/4's aerodynamic downforce on the grid a few minutes before the start. 'Ayrton will now be World Champion,' conceded Prost, 'and I think he fully deserves it. He has driven extremely well this season. He will be a worthy champion.'

In retrospect, Prost's declaration seems somewhat melodramatic. A few weeks later he confessed that he'd been suffering from mid-season blues, grappling with an intermittently troublesome engine and a chassis which definitely didn't feel up to scratch. Moreover, who could have foreseen, on that sunny afternoon, as Senna mastered the high-speed sweeps of Spa-Francorchamps, that the Brazilian would be away from the winner's circle for the next two months?

Monza, of course, was the one spectacular flaw in the McLaren team's otherwise impeccable display. Ayrton took the lead from the start, with Prost chasing hard, already handicapped by a slightly misfiring engine, but at least consoling himself with the fact that he had been allocated a brand new chassis for this race. Alain was eventually to retire with a rare piston failure. By this time the McLaren team-mates had raced each other into a parlous fuel situation, leaving Senna with the prospect of scraping home by a hair's breadth from the Ferraris – assuming he took the absolute maximum out of the chassis and pussy-footed with his throttle control.

That historic moment when Jean-Louis Schlesser, in the Williams, collided with Senna at the first chicane, with fractionally less than two laps left to run, will be etched in the minds of Grand Prix fans for a generation. Even Ron Dennis allowed that it had been a demonstration of the way in which Senna's supreme confidence and push in traffic could work against him. Moreover, the strategic need to shimmer through this particular gap with a sense of total urgency was of paramount importance to the race's potential outcome. Some you win, some you lose.

Its run of eleven consecutive victories broken by that Monza misfortune, the McLaren team regrouped at Estoril for the Portuguese Grand Prix, determined to restore the status quo. This time Prost started from pole position, Ayrton finding that his MP4/4's cockpit instruments were playing up through much of qualifying. There were two starts to this race, the first aborted by a multiple shunt down among the midfield runners. In the sprint to the first corner, meanwhile, Prost eased out Senna with untypical spirit, almost pushing the Brazilian onto the grass on the left-hand side of the circuit as he took the line into the turn.

Senna was not impressed. At the second start, when Alain attempted to duplicate the manoeuvre, Ayrton held him out and chopped across into the lead. Then, as Alain hurtled up onto his tail, coming out of the last right-hander to complete the opening lap, Ayrton squeezed him towards the pit wall in what was, by any standards, an extremely hazardous piece of driving. Prost kept his nerve, though, his MP4/4 skipping precariously over the bumps as he surged by into the lead. The Frenchman was never headed all the way to the flag. Ayrton, battling with poor chassis balance and blistered tyres (which forced a pit stop after contact with Mansell's Williams), finished sixth.

The two men resolved their differences over that first-lap incident behind closed doors, Prost telling Ayrton that, frankly, he hadn't really appreciated how much he wanted to win the championship. In fact, Alain told him, he could take it if it meant driving like that. Ayrton was briefly chastened, but steadfastly refused to answer press enquiries about the exchange. 'It's over, forgotten,' he said firmly. Ron Dennis tried to appear relaxed about the episode, although he was clearly concerned. 'You've got to remember it's not a schoolgirls' tea party out there,' he told me. 'They are racing for the World Championship, for heaven's sake . . .' Even so, it had been too close for comfort.

A week later, Prost dominated the Spanish Grand Prix at Jerez, leading from start to finish despite the fact that Ayrton had qualified in pole position. The Brazilian wound up fourth, his fuel computer providing him with unnecessarily pessimistic information for much of the race. Speculation now centred on whether or not Prost could sustain his slender advantage in the points table, bearing in mind that, under the 'best 11 out of 16' results rule, he was only amassing three points for each win from Spain onwards. Senna was mathematically in the stronger position.

On Sunday, 30 October 1988, Ayrton finally stamped his irrevocable authority on that season's battle for the World Championship with a quite remarkable victory in the Japanese Grand Prix at Suzuka. Not that Prost proved a pushover, in fact far from it.

*Leading Ivan Capelli's Leyton House March in the
1988 Portuguese Grand Prix at Estoril. It was a bad day
for Ayrton and he trailed home sixth, hamstrung by
heavy fuel consumption.*

*Senna seizes the lead of the 1988 Japanese Grand Prix
at Suzuka, sweeping past Prost as the two McLarens
lap the Rial of Andrea de Cesaris.*

Despite having to endure an upset stomach for much of practice, he qualified second alongside Senna and believed he could have been in pole position but for a missed gearchange.

Then, when the starting lights blinked to green, Prost was presented with a once-in-a-lifetime bonus. Senna jerked forward and stalled the engine. Gerhard Berger's Ferrari fish-tailed past the near-stationary McLaren to the left, Nelson Piquet's Lotus 100T dived to the right. By the thickness of a coat of paint they both avoided making contact.

Aided by the downhill slope on which the Suzuka startline is positioned, Ayrton found he had just enough momentum to bump the McLaren back into life. But the engine stalled for a second time before he finally, successfully, coaxed it back onto full song. But by now Prost had the race in the bag. Or so it seemed.

Alain completed the opening 3.642-mile lap comfortably ahead of the Ferraris of Berger and Michele Alboreto. Senna, 12th into the first corner, was now eighth. He was seventh on lap two, sixth on lap three, yet didn't seem to be making ground on Prost at the sort of rate required to get a winning job done in front of the madly enthusiastic Japanese crowd on this day at Suzuka.

Yet the intervention of a slight rain shower eventually tipped the balance in Senna's favour. Running on slicks in the damp was definitely not to Prost's taste and he eased his pace to the point that Ivan Capelli's Leyton House March briefly drew alongside and nosed ahead as they crossed the start/finish line on lap 16. The McLaren-Honda's sheer power enabled Alain to hold the advantage into the first corner, but the track conditions had by now deteriorated to the point that Senna was carving relentlessly into his advantage.

Prost, moreover, found himself increasingly hampered by slight gearchange problems, missing the odd shift here and there. At the end of the 27th lap he was balked by the Rial of Andrea de Cesaris at the tight chicane before the pits. It was all Senna needed to launch a perfectly judged dive up the inside of his team-mate as they stormed into the fast right-hander after the pits. Prost gave Senna precisely the room he required and not a millimetre more. That was all he needed.

Senna initially pulled out a five-second advantage and a brief counter-attack by Prost was thwarted by some appallingly obstructive driving on the part of some slower cars. Ayrton eventually won by just over 13 seconds, taking the chequered flag as a rain shower doused the circuit for the second time during the afternoon.

Senna had not only clinched his first World Championship title, but established a new record of eight wins in a single season. The previous record of seven wins had been set by the late Jim Clark, at the wheel of a Lotus-Coventry Climax, as long ago as 1963. Another 21 years passed before Alain Prost equalled it and now it had been excelled by Ayrton Senna, the third Brazilian after Emerson Fittipaldi and Nelson Piquet to grasp the World Championship title.

*Once ahead, Ayrton made no mistake, clinching the
World Championship with his eighth win of the season.*

Prost was clearly disappointed to have lost out in the battle for the championship so late in the day. But at least he could console himself with the thought that he knew what made Senna tick, that he understood his team-mate. His assessment at the end of 1988 makes fascinating reading in the light of what was to come.

'What impressed me was his ability to push hard at all times and be quick in all conditions,' said the Frenchman. 'It doesn't matter whether it's a fast or slow circuit, rain or heat or traffic . . . he has an enormously high degree of commitment.

'Our relationship has been better than perhaps I might have imagined; a bit tense to start with, but progressively improving – with one or two exceptions – through to the end of the year. But I always knew that 1988 might be difficult because he wanted the World Championship so passionately, just as I did the first time. Even now, in Adelaide, I sense that he is more relaxed now he has achieved his ambition.'

In fact, Prost had got it very largely wrong. The 1988 season had been difficult because of Senna's utterly uncompromising commitment to victory at all costs. If Alain believed life would somehow be easier, less stressed, in 1989 he was totally incorrect. From Senna's viewpoint, his own success in the 1988 title battle had been the first step towards destroying Prost as a rival.

There was nothing overtly personal in this; Alain was the man most likely to stand between Ayrton and the distinction of being statistically the most successful driver of all time. So the Frenchman had to be dealt with. If Alain had known about a conversation which had taken place more than a year earlier between Ayrton and former McLaren driver John Watson, he would have received a clearer insight into Senna's long-term strategy.

Watson had attended a dinner party in Germany hosted by Mercedes-Benz public relations man Gerd Kramer during which he struck up a conversation with Senna. The Brazilian was working out his final season at Team Lotus prior to joining McLaren for 1988, so the discussion inevitably turned to the subject of Ayrton's future prospects. In particular, they chatted about how Ayrton would handle going into a team with such a strong, established driver as Alain Prost.

Watson offered his own opinion that the best way of beating Prost would be by stealth rather than a head-to-head confrontation. Ayrton listened with all due deference and then told John that he had other ideas.

'He told me that he would beat Prost by being fitter, more motivated and more dedicated,' recalls Watson. 'He said that he would make sure that he was in a position to drive faster and more consistently, for longer than Prost could do. He meant to beat him convincingly from the front. I remember thinking that was a little optimistic.'

Ayrton proved an outstandingly adept F1 newcomer during his novice year in 1984, starting out with the Toleman TG183B.

Right: *Winning his first Detroit Grand Prix with the JPS Lotus 98T-Renault.*

*Fending off Mansell's Williams on the last corner at
Jerez, 1986.*

*Practising the Lotus 99T-Honda in the rain for the 1987
Belgian Grand Prix.*

*Overleaf: Ayrton scored a record eight wins in 1988 to
clinch his first World Championship at the wheel of the
McLaren MP4/4.*

Ayrton leading Prost and the Ferraris of Berger and Alboreto in the early stages of the 1988 Belgian Grand Prix.

Ayrton and Alain: getting along fine, for the moment.

Opposite: *Senna is the embodiment of concentration and commitment, even away from the circuits.*

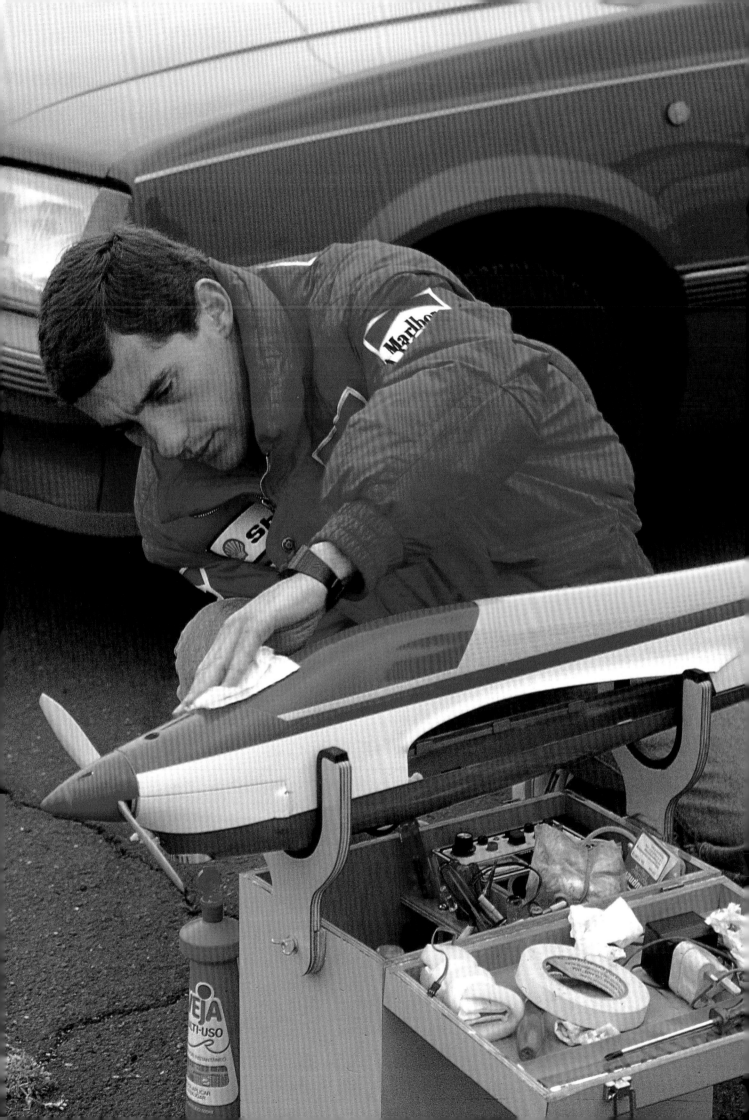

Leading Pierluigi Martini's Minardi shortly after the start of the rain-soaked 1989 Australian Grand Prix, which would be won by Boutsen's Williams after Ayrton ran into the back of Martin Brundle's Brabham.

Running ahead of Alain Prost in the 1989 Mexican Grand Prix. By now personal relations between the two men had become untenable.

Phoenix, 1990: a winning performance.

The lowest moment of Ayrton's career. His McLaren
and Prost's Ferrari plunge off the circuit at Suzuka
following their first-corner collision in the 1990
Japanese Grand Prix.

Monaco in 1991: another
brilliant performance in
the McLaren MP4/6 to
make it four wins from
the first four races of the
season.

Good pals. Ayrton got on
well with his new team-
mate Gerhard Berger,
who succeeded Prost at
the start of 1990.

Not at all. Having won the '88 championship, Ayrton set about making the title his personal property in perpetuity. For 1989 the F1 regulations were framed for 3.5-litre naturally aspirated cars and, with Honda producing the first-ever V10 to be used for competition purposes, there seemed little likelihood of anybody seriously challenging McLaren when it came to making a run for the World Championship.

From the start of the 1989 season, Senna became more introspective – at least as far as Prost was concerned. Eventually Alain concluded, 'He thrives on conflict, whereas I am the opposite . . .' It was his most shrewd assessment of his relationship with the Brazilian to date.

Yet Senna still displayed an irrepressible streak of impetuosity. It was almost as if he couldn't bring himself to believe that anybody could show signs of beating him, let alone actually complete the job. It was an approach which almost added up to disaster at the first corner of the first race, on Ayrton's home turf in Brazil.

Senna had planted the McLaren MP4/5 on pole position, but Riccardo Patrese's Williams FW12-Renault got the jump on him when the green lights went on. The Williams drew level with the McLaren on the left just as Gerhard Berger's Ferrari 640, its fast start aided by the speedy shifts from its electro-hydraulic gearchange, came up on Senna's right.

Neck and neck the three cars sprinted for the first corner, Ayrton unwilling to concede. In the resultant collision Berger spun and the McLaren lost its nose section. The race was won by Nigel Mansell's Ferrari with Prost second and Mauricio Gugelmin's March third. Ayrton finished 11th, two laps down, after a total of four pit stops for fresh tyres and bodywork checks.

The trouble between Prost and Senna really began to well up at the second round of the World Championship. Ayrton suggested a deal to Prost whereby the two McLarens would not race each other through the first corner at Imola, venue for the San Marino Grand Prix. There was to be no repeat of the Rio débâcle; whichever of them arrived at the corner first would be permitted by the other to proceed unmolested.

At the start, Senna got away cleanly. However, the race was red-flagged to a halt following a major accident to Gerhard Berger's Ferrari, and the restart was not destined to go so smoothly. This time, Prost got the jump on Senna and led down towards Tosa. But Ayrton found himself unable to adhere to the terms of his own proposal and ducked past under braking, going through a gap which Prost had left open in all innocence, believing his colleague would keep his side of the bargain.

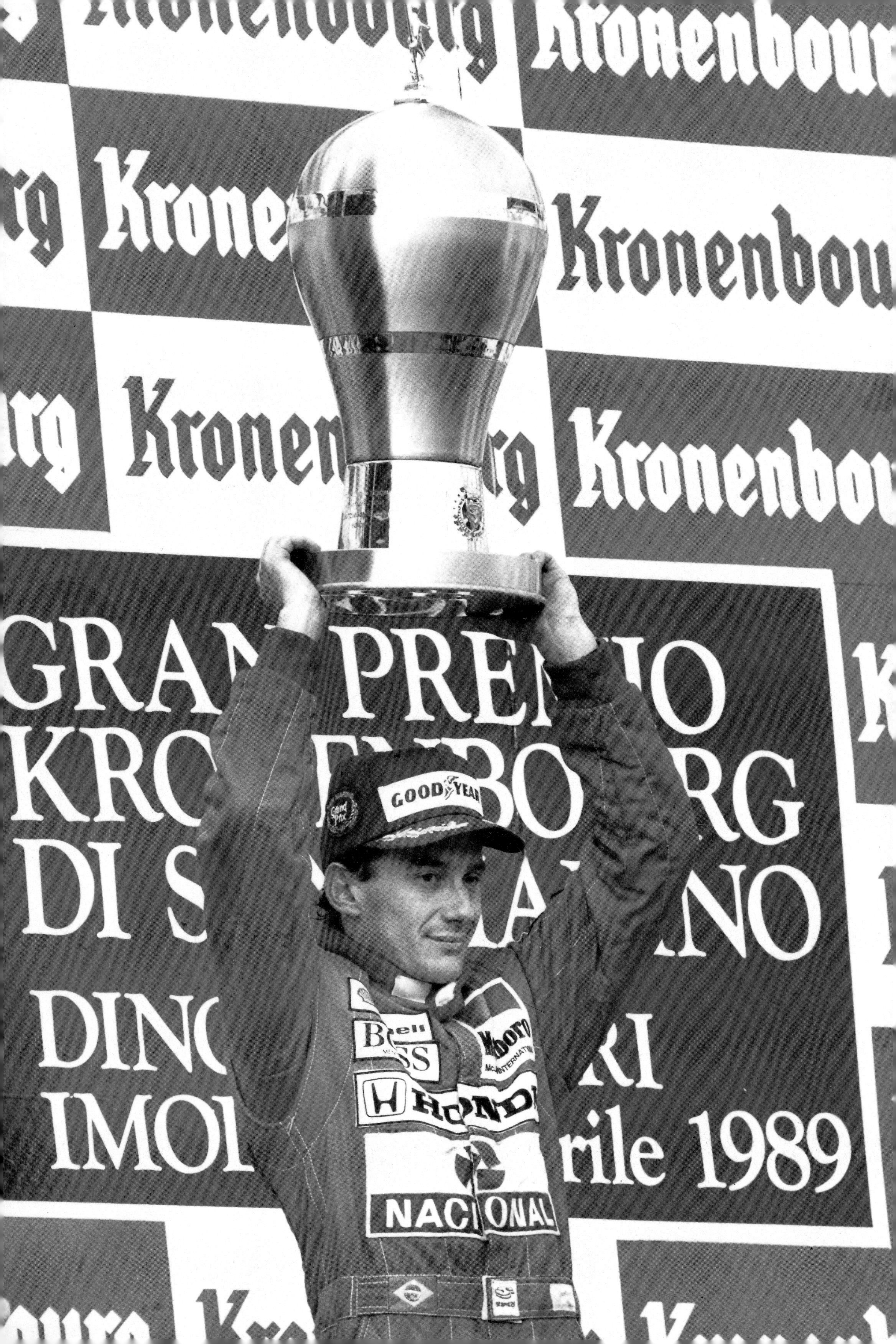
GOODYEAR
NACIONAL

*On the rostrum at Imola after the race which caused his
first serious breach with Alain Prost.*

*The two McLaren MP4/5s in close company during
that controversial San Marino GP.*

Nevertheless, the two McLarens finished the race in commanding 1-2 formation, but Prost was furious. In his anger, he failed to turn up at the post-race press conference, a misdemeanour for which he was fined $5000. He was outraged by what he regarded as Senna's duplicity and, privately, even more angry that he had allowed himself to be taken in.

In retrospect, Senna was willingly handing Prost the tools with which psychologically to bury himself. At the next race, Monaco, McLaren boss Ron Dennis intervened in this private dispute between his two drivers, as a result of which Ayrton apologised to Prost during a subsequent test session at Pembrey. 'In future, I will be part of any plan or arrangement the drivers might make,' said Dennis commandingly.

It had been a bruising experience for Prost, compounded by the way in which Ayrton totally defeated him in another McLaren demonstration run through the streets of the Principality. At Mexico City, Senna kept up the pressure. He made the correct choice of tyres and scored his third win of the season. Prost didn't and finished fourth after two pit stops. Alain also began to feel that some Honda V10 engines were more equal than others.

Electrical trouble intervened to thwart Senna's efforts in the inaugural Phoenix Grand Prix, but again he was ahead of Alain before encountering his problems. As a result, Prost was able to notch up his first win of the season, moving back into a two-point championship lead. Then everything suddenly seemed to go wrong for Ayrton.

His domination of the rain-soaked Canadian Grand Prix was thwarted by engine failure only three laps from the finish. This was a rare event for McLaren, who recorded retirements with both cars, Prost stopping when a front suspension pick-up point began pulling out of the monocoque. But Alain took a commanding win at Paul Ricard when Senna's car broke its transmission at the start and the Brazilian then threw away victory at Silverstone with a fumbled gearchange that saw his car end up firmly embedded in a sand trap. Alain inherited that victory as well and had consolidated a majestic 20-point advantage at the head of the championship table.

Prost plays McLaren second fiddle to Senna at Monaco,
1989.

Yet, behind the scenes, Senna had already won a significant victory. Confused and unsettled, Prost had been unable to offer a continuing commitment to McLaren for 1990 when approached to do so by Ron Dennis and TAG boss Mansour Ojjeh. He decided to leave the team. A few weeks later, Dennis announced that Gerhard Berger would be filling the vacant seat in the McLaren line-up for 1990. Ayrton had not only sapped Prost's morale, but driven him out of his spiritual home. Dennis would later remark that it was a matter of regret that he was 'unable to create a situation where these two top drivers could operate together within the same team'.

Gradually Senna inched into Prost's championship advantage with wins at Hockenheim, Spa – a peerless performance in torrential rain – and Spain. But it was a far from perfect canvas. Monza had been blighted by an engine failure, Estoril by a collision with Mansell's Ferrari after Ayrton had attempted to close the door on the Englishman and the two cars pirouetted at high speed into the sand trap at the first corner. 'He could have killed me,' said Ayrton, resolutely declining to accept any responsibility for the incident.

All these upsets meant that Ayrton went into the Japanese Grand Prix some 16 points behind Prost. The complexities of the points scoring system were such that he now had to win both at Suzuka and in the final race a fortnight later in Adelaide.

Senna tackled the task of qualifying at Suzuka with his customary zeal, taking pole position by over a second from Prost. But when it came to the race, Alain gambled on a low-downforce aerodynamic set-up which gave his car the edge over Senna's. In addition, with pole position at Suzuka being off the racing line, Prost had the benefit of the extra grip on the left-hand side of the circuit from which to launch himself straight into the lead at the start of the race.

What followed was a classic chase between two great racing drivers. Prost apparently had the upper hand on this day, whether through inspired driving, a car that was working slightly better, or a bit of both. The status quo was sustained throughout their routine tyre stops, but with six laps to go Senna made a superhuman effort under braking for the tight chicane just prior to the pits.

Superhuman. Or reckless. The precise interpretation depends on the individual's assessment of Senna as a racing driver. Those who believe he is faultless, one of the greatest of all time, favour the former description. Others who feel he displays a uniquely flawed genius opt for the latter verdict. Either way the end result was the same.

The worm had turned. Two years of Prost putting up with Ayrton's intimidatory tactics had finally come to an end. With an almost naïve lack of subtlety, Alain closed the door on his team-mate. The two McLaren-Hondas slithered to an ignominious halt, locked together, under the noses of the Honda top brass. It was pure farce.

However, while Prost undid his belts and vacated the cockpit, Senna motioned the marshals to push-start his car. But instead of turning back to negotiate the chicane, he aimed his McLaren down the escape road and back onto the track. He then drove brilliantly to retake the lead from Alessandro Nannini's Benetton after a lightning pit stop in which the McLaren mechanics replaced the damaged nose section with astonishing despatch. Yet Ayrton was disqualified for going through the chicane, not round it. Prost was World Champion.

McLaren predictably appealed against the sentence, but when the team's representatives turned up in Paris the following Friday for the hearing, they were stunned to be presented with a savage indictment of Senna's driving style. Every questionable incident in which he had been involved throughout the 1989 season was laid out in a dossier which not only accused him of breaching the rules at Suzuka, but also of a series of misjudgements and errors which had no bearing on the main issue.

The Court of Appeal deferred its decision until the following week, eventually upholding Senna's exclusion from the race and imposing a $100,000 fine together with a six-month suspended ban. McLaren were so outraged at their driver's treatment that they even threatened a civil action against FISA unless the appeal hearing was successful.

This was a fruitless avenue to pursue, but it reflected the feeling of overwhelming personal devastation which Senna emotionally projected to the media on the eve of the Australian Grand Prix. Fighting back the tears, here was a man who passionately believed, from the bottom of his heart, that he had been wronged. This was the most aggressive and motivated front-line Grand Prix driver of his era in a head-to-head confrontation with the sporting authority.

At the time, it seemed there was every possibility that he might retire from the sport. 'I will fight to the end this unjust penalty,' he insisted. How precisely he could take the matter any further was not explained, however.

Yet the manner in which Senna attacked the Australian Grand Prix was quite remarkable. In his mind, he was going for the World Championship. Had the events at Suzuka gone to plan, had he won the race without question, he could hardly have set about the Adelaide street circuit with more motivation.

In appalling torrential rain he tackled the final round of the title chase with a Messianic zeal which ended only when he slammed into the back of Martin Brundle's Brabham, which had been groping its way along, enveloped in a cloud of spray. Both drivers were extremely fortunate to have suffered no injury.

In the wake of this incident, Senna then made one of the most remarkable observations

Carefully thinking about how to frame a response to a questioner at a press conference during 1989.

of his entire career. Having conceded that the amount of water on the surface had increased dramatically after the first few laps, he added: 'By the time I had my accident, the conditions were no longer acceptable. From that moment they should have stopped the race. The championship was no longer an issue because I was out. There was no more pressure on anybody.'

On the face of it, the disdainful belief that the outcome of the World Championship was the only factor that was of any consequence throughout a year of F1 endeavour was hard to take. But there was something simplistic about his benevolent concern for his rivals in these circumstances. The remarks were an almost unconscious manifestation of his superiority complex as a racing driver.

After Adelaide, Ayrton returned to Brazil for the winter. Back home, his bitterness spilled over. He accused FISA President Jean-Marie Balestre of having manipulated the outcome of the championship in Prost's favour. It looked as though Ayrton was prepared to commit career suicide for his principles. Despite being summoned in front of the World Motor Sports Council during the winter, he refused to atone and remained unrepentant. His $100,000 fine remained unpaid.

In the end, Senna had to climb down, pay up and withdraw his allegations before he was permitted to take part in the 1990 World Championship. He appeared at the opening round at Phoenix with the winter's tension still preying on his mind. He won the race, but confessed he had derived little satisfaction from doing so. Only the warm-hearted spontaneity of his fans when he arrived at Interlagos for the Brazilian Grand Prix helped him to feel comfortable with the Formula 1 business again.

Ayrton failed to win in front of his beloved home crowd, tangling with Nakajima before finishing third behind Prost, now his personal nemesis, and his new McLaren partner Gerhard Berger. It took until Monaco for him to slot into his customary devastating winning ways, then he reeled off a commanding victory in Montreal before the McLaren steamroller suffered a very significant mid-season drop-off in form.

Prost's Ferrari rattled off three wins in succession but an intensive programme of chassis improvements enabled Ayrton to put the MP4/5B back on the competitive high wire at Hockenheim, a race from which he emerged with a four-point advantage over Prost in the championship points table. Second place at the Hungaroring, followed by victories at Spa and Monza, seemed to consolidate the position. There even seemed to be time to make up with Prost. On the face of it.

At the post-race press conference at Monza, where Ayrton was sharing the top table with both Prost and Berger, a journalist asked whether they would ever bury the

A rear shot of Ayrton's MP4/5B at Monaco in 1990,
showing off its distinctive arched diffuser panels.

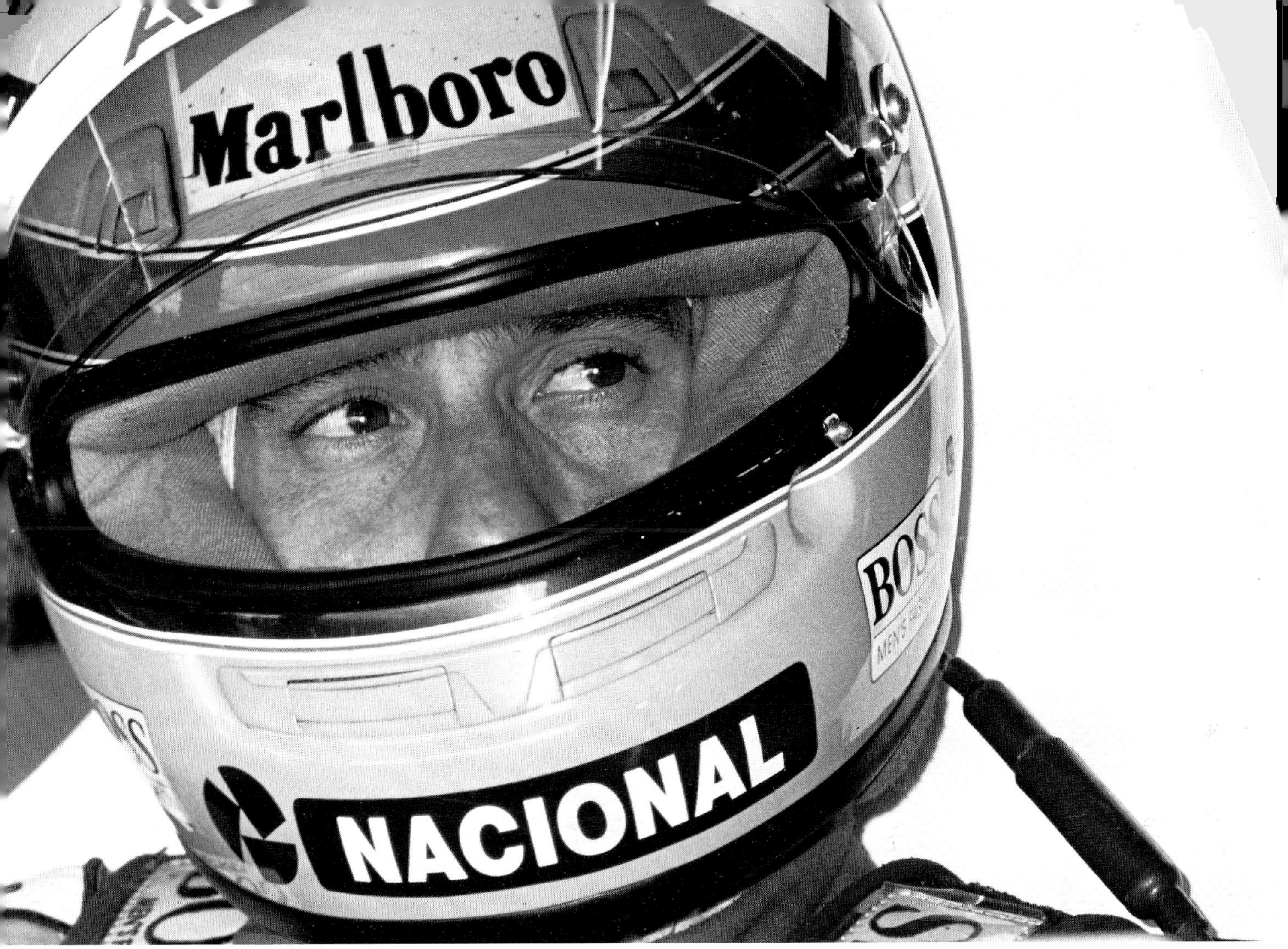
Marlboro
BOSS
NACIONAL

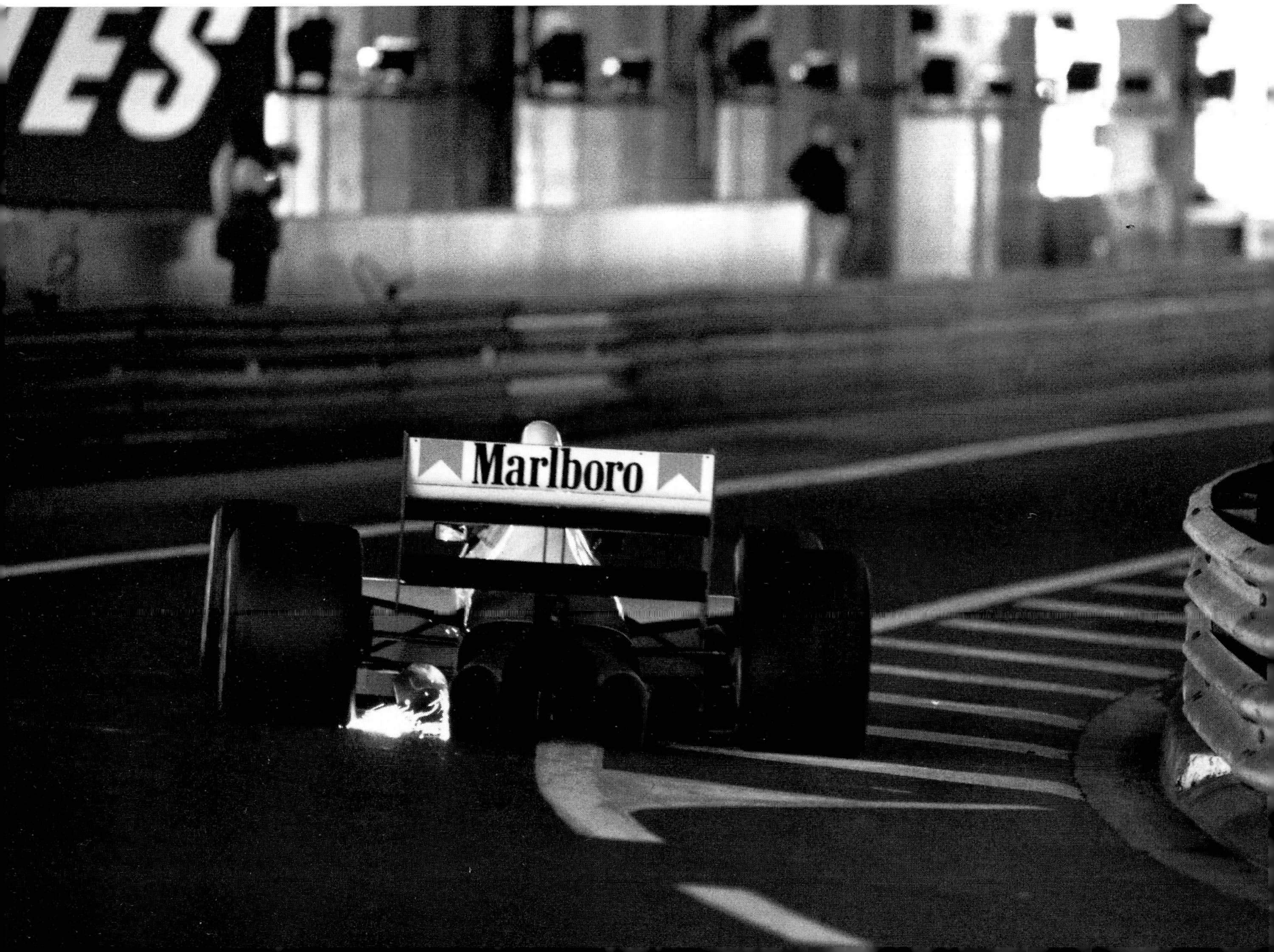
Marlboro

Leading Berger during the early stages of the 1990
Italian Grand Prix at Monza with the over-exuberant
Jean Alesi just about to spin his Tyrrell into retirement
as they negotiate the first chicane after the pits.

hatchet. Under the arc lights, Prost offered his hand to Ayrton. Hesitantly, Senna took it. 'It's a beginning,' he conceded. But he didn't look comfortable. And he didn't look convinced, either.

What was slipping into pin-sharp focus throughout the 1990 season was Senna's ruthless loyalty to himself, reflecting a trait which seems particularly well developed in Brazilians. Life for Ayrton is about fierce, protective loyalty to his family circle and a few close friends. The rest of the world, particularly within motor racing, is fair game to be played like a Stradivarius.

He could be friendly enough, on the surface at least, with other drivers who didn't pose a threat. But they were the enemy and whatever might have taken place in the paddock – a friendly chat or some rare, lighthearted horseplay – had absolutely nothing to do with what happened on the circuit.

Of course, the history books will show that Ayrton clinched the 1990 World Championship when he dived inside Prost as they attacked the first corner at Suzuka. The ensuing collision sparked world-wide controversy, with the McLaren team dutifully lining up to support their driver's case, blaming the fact that pole position had not been moved to the left-hand side of the circuit to avoid the dusty line, and so on.

Ayrton had to settle for runner-up slot at the
Hungaroring for the second successive year in 1990,
beaten this time by Thierry Boutsen's Williams.

Others, such as Jackie Stewart and Niki Lauda, declared that Senna was totally out of order. Prost was speechless. The apparent rapprochement at Monza had counted for nothing. Senna was unabashed by all the attention. 'The World Championship is won over a full season, not at an individual race,' he stated. It was a viewpoint which seemed conveniently to overlook the fact that his driving tactics had been the factor to prevent Prost having a full 16-race season to contest that self-same title.

Ayrton's confidence received a further boost when he renewed his contract for 1991 with the McLaren team at the end of its initial three-year spell. It was clearly a very lucrative deal indeed, agreement on which had only been reached after he had talked long and hard with Williams. In some ways, it is hard to resist the conclusion that Senna was wasting everybody's time with these negotiations and that there was never much chance of him leaving McLaren and Honda. But, in his own individualistic way, he kept everybody guessing until the last minute.

After another winter spent recharging his batteries in Brazil, Ayrton reappeared at the wheel of the brand new McLaren MP4/6 at the start of the 1991 season to pick up the thread of his winning ways once more. Despite advising Honda that the winter's development programme on the new V12 engine had simply not made sufficient progress in terms of power output, Ayrton opened the year by reeling off four consecutive victories at Phoenix, Interlagos, Imola and Monaco.

The sweetest success came in front of his home crowd in São Paulo, of course, where he at last won the Brazilian Grand Prix after an effort which was heroic even by his own high standards. Grappling with serious gearbox problems, running on slicks with a light rain shower falling, Ayrton's physical exhaustion at the finish was such that he had to be helped from the McLaren's cockpit after taking the chequered flag.

*Grappling with dire gearbox problems, Ayrton
struggles towards victory in the '91 Brazilian Grand
Prix.*

Those four wins gave him a crucial early points advantage to cushion himself against the burgeoning challenge from the Williams-Renaults. The Honda V12 just wasn't in the same league as the Renault V10 – to start with, at least. Yet Senna now displayed a steady hand, a maturity of purpose, which helped him to pick up consistently high results even when the MP4/6 was off the pace. The most notable of these was at Mexico City where, having rolled the car at the daunting banked Peralta right-hander in practice, he finished third behind the Williams-Renault duo.

Ayrton's composure even remained intact when the McLaren ran out of fuel on the last lap at both Silverstone and Hockenheim due to problems with an incorrectly calibrated fuel read-out. Perhaps his equanimity was helped by the knowledge that a much-improved engine would be available for the Hungarian Grand Prix, installed in a lightened MP4/6 chassis.

The Hockenheim race produced more conflict between Senna and Prost, with Alain complaining vehemently about what he regarded as the Brazilian's unethical driving tactics while he was close behind him. Senna dismissed the Frenchman's protests with contempt, but the tension between the two men remained as intense as ever.

At Budapest, Senna capitalised superbly on the potential of the revised McLaren, going straight into the lead from pole position, never to be headed. Mansell and Patrese both tried to mount a challenge, but there was no question of overtaking unless Ayrton made a mistake. And none was forthcoming.

Opposite top: *Resisting the challenge from Mansell's*
Williams during the 1991 Hungarian Grand Prix, a
turning-point in Ayrton's quest for his third
championship.

Senna and Prost discussed their differences at length
during a private meeting in the Hungaroring paddock,
offering renewed hope of an end to their long-running
feud. The occasion was marked in style in the Elf
hospitality area (inset), *but the media attention*
remained unrelenting.

Cocktails!
Hungarian
rhapsody
(sans l'alcool)
Senna -"-
Prost
SURPRISE

A fortnight later Ayrton won at Spa after Mansell encountered trouble, and he finished a brilliantly judged second to the Englishman at Monza after a tactical drive, hanging on ahead of the Williams and then making a quick stop for fresh tyres the instant Mansell forced his way past. Another tactical second place, this time to Riccardo Patrese – Mansell having been disqualified after a disastrously fumbled tyre change – followed in the Portuguese Grand Prix at Estoril, the Williams FW14 now demonstrating a clear edge over the McLaren almost everywhere they raced.

At this stage, Ayrton began to take umbrage over what he regarded as Mansell's over-aggressive driving style, complaining about the way in which the Williams driver had stormed past both McLarens going into the first corner at Estoril.

'Perhaps I let him have it a little too easy,' said Ayrton ominously. 'If it had been any other race I would have let the accident happen.' This was an extraordinary attitude to take. Ayrton Senna suddenly complaining about intimidatory tactics hardly had the ring of veracity about it. More than anybody else in the sport's recent history, Senna had been responsible for legitimising such tactics in Formula 1.

Ayrton's complaints about Mansell continued the following weekend at Barcelona's new Circuit de Catalunya, where the Spanish Grand Prix was being held for the first time. Yet nobody else could see what foundation existed for his complaints, least of all the obscene verbal outburst he aimed at the Englishman during the official drivers' briefing.

He followed this up with a lacklustre race to fifth place, having made the wrong choice of tyres and performed inconsistently. Everybody can have an off-day, but it is a measure of Ayrton Senna's sustained high standards that such an event provokes amazement verging on disbelief.

However, there were technical improvements in the pipeline which enabled McLaren and Honda to raise their game in time for the Japanese Grand Prix at Suzuka. With significant aerodynamic improvements to the chassis, even more power from a further-lightened Honda V12, which was itself benefiting from further Shell fuel developments, Berger and Senna took the first two places on the starting grid with Mansell's Williams the only other contender in the same league.

With two races left to go, Senna was leading Mansell by 16 points and thus, with a maximum of only 20 points remaining to be won, needed only five more points to put his third championship beyond challenge, even if Mansell was to win both the remaining Grands Prix. Prior to the start of the race it was agreed that whichever McLaren

*Holding off Mansell's Williams FW14 through the 'bus
stop' chicane at the 1991 Belgian Grand Prix, on a day
when Ayrton was lucky and Nigel was not!*

Opposite: *Sharing his delight at winning the
championship with 1991 Japanese Grand Prix winner
Gerhard Berger, after Ayrton had delivered victory into
the Austrian's hands by conceding the race almost on the
finishing line. Patrese* (right) *completes the trio.*

*Winner takes all: Ayrton at the post-race press
conference in Adelaide, 1991.*

was ahead after two laps would be allowed to win.

At the start Gerhard made a faultless getaway to lead through the first right-hander and, with Ayrton keeping Mansell at bay, the Austrian quickly pulled away from the pack. Going into the tenth lap, Mansell spun off into the sand trap at the corner which, a year earlier, had seen Prost tangle with Senna. Ayrton was now World Champion for the third time.

Freed of the need to drive a tactical race, Senna now piled on the pressure to take the lead from Berger before they made their routine tyre stops. Riccardo Patrese's Williams then led briefly before making its own tyre stop, allowing Senna and Berger to retake first and second positions.

As he exited the chicane on the final lap, Ayrton pulled over to the left and waved Gerhard by to take the win, as previously arranged. 'It hurt a lot, believe me,' he grinned afterwards, 'but it was a small gesture to Gerhard who has helped me this year, and I mean a small one, because he was certainly as quick as me here this afternoon.'

However, at the post-race press conference, Ayrton stood the world on its ear. He suddenly decided to unburden himself on the subject of the previous two Suzuka races: the 1989 event when he believed he was wrongly disqualified and the 1990 race where he clashed with Prost at the first corner. What he had to say was sensational on two counts.

In an extraordinarily profane outburst, he savaged former FISA President Jean-Marie Balestre, blaming the Frenchman for interfering in both races.

Of his 1989 disqualification, he said, 'I had won the race and was prevented from going to the podium by Jean-Marie Balestre. I was robbed badly by the system and that I will never forget.'

Strong stuff. But it was as nothing compared to his revelation that, yes, in fact he *had* pushed Prost's Ferrari off the road a year later on the first corner. Again he blamed Balestre for interfering with the organisers' original intention to move pole position over to the left-hand side of the track so that the fastest qualifier had the benefit of the cleaner, racing line.

*Final win of '91. Ayrton trailed by Mansell in the rain-
soaked Adelaide débâcle which was flagged to a halt
after 14 precarious laps.*

'The officials had said, "No problem, we put pole position on the outside,"' he explained, 'and then Balestre intervened and said, "No, we don't think so." This was really shit. I said, OK, you try to do your job properly and you get f★★★★★ many times by stupid people. So I said if, on Sunday, Prost gets ahead of me off the grid he'd better not turn in ahead of me because he's not going to make it.

'I really wish it hadn't happened. It was a shit end to the championship. It wasn't good for me and it wasn't good for Formula 1. It was a result of wrong decisions and partiality by those on the inside. I won the championship, but so what? It had been a bad example for everybody.'

Ayrton Senna had been part of the Grand Prix community for eight years by the end of the 1991 season, yet he remained probably the most private of all top-line drivers. He is now wary about relationships, reluctant for people to get too close in case they betray his trust. There are no half-measures with Senna. You are either with him or against him. It's black or white. A reasoned debate about his talent, his shortcomings, is not generally appreciated.

Prior to the 1991 Japanese Grand Prix he had accumulated 32 victories in World Championship races, second only to Alain Prost's tally of 44 wins. Nobody could dispute his unusual commitment to his chosen sport, or his status as one of the greatest Grand Prix drivers of all time.

Yet, in many ways, he is an odd mixture of contradictions. He sets great store by good manners, yet can be breathtakingly off-hand. He projects cool equanimity, yet a Latin temperament – and temper – lurk close to the surface. He has come to be regarded as the definitive talent of his time, yet reveals his human side with the occasional fundamental error on the track.

Of course, Senna the driver is only part of the complex equation which makes up the complete man. Away from the track he can be cordial and has the capacity to project his very high intellect through a quite remarkable grasp of the English language. He is charming and generous to children, something which is probably a manifestation of his strong family bonding.

There are also other instances of his private charity which have recently been brought to the author's attention by people who wish to remain anonymous, but throw light onto a gentle, caring aspect to Ayrton Senna's character which may not always be apparent in the hard-bitten world of the Formula 1 pit lane.

Yet, at the end of the day, Ayrton Senna is his own sternest taskmaster. His high standards and devotion to driving excellence spur him on to ever-greater achievements. Above all else, racing is of no interest to him. Winning is the only, overwhelming priority.

AYRTON SENNA · CAREER RECORD
BY JOHN TAYLOR
AND JOCELYNE BIA

Kart Championship wins	Kart World Championship positions	
1977 South American Championship	1977	6th
1978 South American Championship	1979	2nd
1978 Brazilian Championship	1980	2nd
1979 Brazilian Championship	1981	4th
1980 Brazilian Championship		
1981 Brazilian Championship		

1981

	Race	Circuit	Date	Entrant	Car	Comment
5	P & O Ferries FF1600, round 1	Brands Hatch	01/03/81	Van Diemen	Van Diemen RF80-Ford	First car race
3	Townsend-Thoresen FF1600, round 1	Thruxton	08/03/81	Van Diemen	Van Diemen RF81-Ford	
1	Townsend-Thoresen FF1600, round 2	Brands Hatch	15/03/81	Van Diemen	Van Diemen RF81-Ford	First win
2	Townsend-Thoresen FF1600, round 3	Mallory Park	22/03/81	Van Diemen	Van Diemen RF81-Ford	Pole
2	Townsend-Thoresen FF1600, round 4	Mallory Park	05/04/81	Van Diemen	Van Diemen RF81-Ford	
2	Townsend-Thoresen FF1600, round 5	Snetterton	03/05/81	Van Diemen	Van Diemen RF81-Ford	Pole
1	RAC FF1600, round 1	Oulton Park	24/05/81	Van Diemen	Van Diemen RF81-Ford	Fastest lap
1	Townsend-Thoresen FF1600, round 6	Mallory Park	25/05/81	Van Diemen	Van Diemen RF81-Ford	
1	Townsend-Thoresen FF1600, round 7	Snetterton	07/06/81	Van Diemen	Van Diemen RF81-Ford	Fastest lap
2	RAC FF1600, round 2	Silverstone	21/06/81	Van Diemen	Van Diemen RF81-Ford	
1	Townsend-Thoresen FF1600, round 8	Oulton Park	27/06/81	Van Diemen	Van Diemen RF81-Ford	Fastest lap
1	RAC FF1600, round 3	Donington Park	04/07/81	Van Diemen	Van Diemen RF81-Ford	Fastest lap
4	RAC FF1600, round 4	Brands Hatch	12/07/81	Van Diemen	Van Diemen RF81-Ford	Fastest lap
1	Townsend-Thoresen FF1600, round 9	Oulton Park	25/07/81	Van Diemen	Van Diemen RF81-Ford	Fastest lap
1	RAC FF1600, round 5	Mallory Park	26/07/81	Van Diemen	Van Diemen RF81-Ford	Fastest lap
1	Townsend-Thoresen FF1600, round 10	Brands Hatch	02/08/81	Van Diemen	Van Diemen RF81-Ford	
1	RAC FF1600, round 6	Snetterton	09/08/81	Van Diemen	Van Diemen RF81-Ford	Fastest lap
1	Townsend-Thoresen FF1600, round 11	Donington Park	15/08/81	Van Diemen	Van Diemen RF81-Ford	
1	Townsend-Thoresen FF1600, round 12	Thruxton	31/08/81	Van Diemen	Van Diemen RF81-Ford	Pole/Fastest lap
2	Townsend-Thoresen FF1600, round 13	Brands Hatch	29/09/81	Van Diemen	Van Diemen RF81-Ford	Fastest lap

1982

	Race	Circuit	Date	Entrant	Car	Comment
1	Pace British FF2000, round 1	Brands Hatch	07/03/82	Rushen Green Racing	Van Diemen RF82-Ford	Pole/Fastest lap
1	Pace British FF2000, round 2	Oulton Park	27/03/82	Rushen Green Racing	Van Diemen RF82-Ford	Pole/Fastest lap
1	Pace British FF2000, round 3	Silverstone	28/03/82	Rushen Green Racing	Van Diemen RF82-Ford	Pole/Fastest lap
1	Pace British FF2000, round 4	Donington Park	04/04/82	Rushen Green Racing	Van Diemen RF82-Ford	Pole/Fastest lap
1	Pace British FF2000, round 5	Snetterton	09/04/82	Rushen Green Racing	Van Diemen RF82-Ford	Pole/Fastest lap
1	Pace British FF2000, round 6	Silverstone	12/04/82	Rushen Green Racing	Van Diemen RF82-Ford	Pole/Fastest lap
ret	EFDA FF2000, round 1	Zolder	18/04/82	Rushen Green Racing	Van Diemen RF82-Ford	Engine/Pole
1	EFDA FF2000, round 2	Donington Park	02/05/82	Rushen Green Racing	Van Diemen RF82-Ford	Pole/Fastest lap
1	Pace British FF2000, round 7	Mallory Park	02/05/82	Rushen Green Racing	Van Diemen RF82-Ford	Fastest lap
ret	EFDA FF2000, round 3	Zolder	09/05/82	Rushen Green Racing	Van Diemen RF82-Ford	Spun off/Pole/Fastest lap
ret	Pace British FF2000, round 8	Oulton Park	30/05/82	Rushen Green Racing	Van Diemen RF82-Ford	Puncture
1	Celebrity Race	Oulton Park	30/05/82		Sunbeam Talbot Ti	Fastest lap
1	Pace British FF2000, round 9	Brands Hatch	31/05/82	Rushen Green Racing	Van Diemen RF82-Ford	Fastest lap
1	Pace British FF2000, round 10	Mallory Park	06/06/82	Rushen Green Racing	Van Diemen RF82-Ford	Fastest lap
1	Pace British FF2000, round 11	Brands Hatch	13/06/82	Rushen Green Racing	Van Diemen RF82-Ford	Fastest lap
ret	EFDA FF2000, round 4	Hockenheim	20/06/82	Rushen Green Racing	Van Diemen RF82-Ford	Accident/Pole
1	Pace British FF2000, round 12	Oulton Park	26/06/82	Rushen Green Racing	Van Diemen RF82-Ford	Fastest lap
1	EFDA FF2000, round 5	Zandvoort	03/07/82	Rushen Green Racing	Van Diemen RF82-Ford	Pole
2	Pace British FF2000, round 13	Snetterton	04/07/82	Rushen Green Racing	Van Diemen RF82-Ford	
1	Pace British FF2000, round 14	Castle Combe	10/07/82	Rushen Green Racing	Van Diemen RF82-Ford	Pole/Fastest lap
1	Pace British FF2000, round 15	Snetterton	01/08/82	Rushen Green Racing	Van Diemen RF82-Ford	Fastest lap
1	EFDA FF2000, round 6	Hockenheim	08/08/82	Rushen Green Racing	Van Diemen RF82-Ford	Pole/Fastest lap
1	EFDA FF2000, round 7	Österreichring	15/08/82	Rushen Green Racing	Van Diemen RF82-Ford	Pole/Fastest lap
1	EFDA FF2000, round 8	Jyllandsring	22/08/82	Rushen Green Racing	Van Diemen RF82-Ford	Pole/Fastest lap
1	Pace British FF2000, round 16	Thruxton	30/08/82	Rushen Green Racing	Van Diemen RF82-Ford	Fastest lap
1	Pace British FF2000, round 17	Silverstone	05/09/82	Rushen Green Racing	Van Diemen RF82-Ford	Fastest lap
1	EFDA FF2000, round 9	Mondello Park	12/09/82	Rushen Green Racing	Van Diemen RF82-Ford	Fastest lap
2	Pace British FF2000, round 20	Brands Hatch	26/09/82	Rushen Green Racing	Van Diemen RF82-Ford	Fastest lap
1	Formula 3 Race	Thruxton	13/11/82	West Surrey Racing	Ralt RT3-Toyota	Pole/Fastest lap

1983

1	Marlboro British F3, round 1	Silverstone	06/03/83	West Surrey Racing	Ralt RT3-Toyota	*Fastest lap*
1	Marlboro British F3, round 2	Thruxton	13/03/83	West Surrey Racing	Ralt RT3-Toyota	*Pole/Fastest lap*
1	Marlboro British F3, round 3	Silverstone	20/03/83	West Surrey Racing	Ralt RT3-Toyota	*Pole/Fastest lap*
1	Marlboro British F3, round 4	Donington Park	27/03/83	West Surrey Racing	Ralt RT3-Toyota	*Pole/Fastest lap*
1	Marlboro British F3, round 5	Thruxton	04/04/83	West Surrey Racing	Ralt RT3-Toyota	*Pole*
1	Marlboro British F3, round 6	Silverstone	24/04/83	West Surrey Racing	Ralt RT3-Toyota	*Pole/Fastest lap*
1	Marlboro British F3, round 7	Thruxton	02/05/83	West Surrey Racing	Ralt RT3-Toyota	*Pole/Fastest lap*
1	Marlboro British F3, round 8	Brands Hatch	08/05/83	West Surrey Racing	Ralt RT3-Toyota	*Pole/Fastest lap*
1	Marlboro British F3, round 9	Silverstone	30/05/83	West Surrey Racing	Ralt RT3-Toyota	*Pole/Fastest lap*
ret	Marlboro British F3, round 10	Silverstone	12/06/83	West Surrey Racing	Ralt RT3-Toyota	*Crashed at chicane*
dns	Marlboro British F3, round 11	Cadwell Park	19/06/83	West Surrey Racing	Ralt RT3-Toyota	*Crashed in practice/Pole*
ret	Marlboro British F3, round 12	Snetterton	03/07/83	West Surrey Racing	Ralt RT3-Toyota	*Crash with Brundle/Fastest lap*
1	Marlboro British F3, round 13	Silverstone	16/07/83	West Surrey Racing	Ralt RT3-Toyota	*Pole/Fastest lap*
2	Marlboro British F3, round 14	Donington Park	24/07/83	West Surrey Racing	Ralt RT3-Toyota	*Pole/Fastest lap*
ret	Marlboro British F3, round 15	Oulton Park	06/08/83	West Surrey Racing	Ralt RT3-Toyota	*Crash with Brundle/Fastest lap*
1	Marlboro British F3, round 16	Silverstone	29/08/83	West Surrey Racing	Ralt RT3-Toyota	*Pole*
ret	Marlboro British F3, round 17	Oulton Park	11/09/83	West Surrey Racing	Ralt RT3-Toyota	*Crash with Brundle/Pole*
ret	Marlboro British F3, round 18	Thruxton	18/09/83	West Surrey Racing	Ralt RT3-Toyota	*Engine/Pole*
2	Marlboro British F3, round 19	Silverstone	02/10/83	West Surrey Racing	Ralt RT3-Toyota	
1	Macau GP	Macau	20/10/83	Marlboro/Teddy Yip	Ralt RT3-Toyota	*Pole/Fastest lap*
1	Marlboro British F3, round 20	Thruxton	27/10/83	West Surrey Racing	Ralt RT3-Toyota	*Pole/Fastest lap*

1984

ret	BRAZILIAN GP	Rio	25/03/84	Toleman Group Motorsport	Toleman TG183B-Hart	*Turbo boost pressure*
6	SOUTH AFRICAN GP	Kyalami	07/04/84	Toleman Group Motorsport	Toleman TG183B-Hart	*First championship point*
6	BELGIAN GP	Zolder	29/04/84	Toleman Group Motorsport	Toleman TG183B-Hart	*6th place, car disqualified*
dnq	SAN MARINO GP	Imola	06/05/84	Toleman Group Motorsport	Toleman TG183B-Hart	*Tyre/Fuel pump problems*
1	Inaugural Saloon Car Race	Nürburgring	12/05/84	Daimler Benz AG	Mercedes Benz 190E	*First race rebuilt circuit*
ret	FRENCH GP	Dijon	20/05/84	Toleman Group Motorsport	Toleman TG184-Hart	*Turbo*
2	MONACO GP	Monte Carlo	03/07/84	Toleman Group Motorsport	Toleman TG184-Hart	*Race stopped/Fastest lap*
7	CANADIAN GP	Montreal	17/06/84	Toleman Group Motorsport	Toleman TG184-Hart	
ret	DETROIT GP	Detroit	24/06/84	Toleman Group Motorsport	Toleman TG184-Hart	*Broken wishbone/Crashed*
ret	DALLAS GP	Dallas	08/07/84	Toleman Group Motorsport	Toleman TG184-Hart	*Driveshaft*
8	Nürburgring 1000 Km	Nürburgring	15/07/84	Reinhold Joest Racing Team	Porsche 956	*Pescarolo/Johansson co-drove*
3	BRITISH GP	Brands Hatch	22/07/84	Toleman Group Motorsport	Toleman TG184-Hart	
ret	GERMAN GP	Hockenheim	05/08/84	Toleman Group Motorsport	Toleman TG184-Hart	*Rear wing/Accident*
ret	AUSTRIAN GP	Österreichring	19/08/84	Toleman Group Motorsport	Toleman TG184-Hart	*Oil pressure*
ret	DUTCH GP	Zandvoort	26/08/84	Toleman Group Motorsport	Toleman TG184-Hart	*Engine*
dns	ITALIAN GP	Monza	09/09/84	Toleman Group Motorsport	Toleman TG184-Hart	*Dropped by team for one race*
ret	EUROPEAN GP	Nürburgring	07/10/84	Toleman Group Motorsport	Toleman TG184-Hart	*Hit Rosberg*
3	PORTUGUESE GP	Estoril	21/10/84	Toleman Group Motorsport	Toleman TG184-Hart	

1985

ret	BRAZILIAN GP	Rio	07/04/85	John Player Team Lotus	Lotus 97T-Renault	*Electrics*
1	PORTUGUESE GP	Estoril	21/04/85	John Player Team Lotus	Lotus 97T-Renault	*Pole/Fastest lap*
7/ret	SAN MARINO GP	Imola	05/05/85	John Player Team Lotus	Lotus 97T-Renault	*Out of fuel/Pole*
ret	MONACO GP	Monte Carlo	19/05/85	John Player Team Lotus	Lotus 97T-Renault	*Engine/Pole*
16	CANADIAN GP	Montreal	16/06/85	John Player Team Lotus	Lotus 97T-Renault	*Pit stop/Fastest lap*
ret	DETROIT GP	Detroit	23/06/85	John Player Team Lotus	Lotus 97T-Renault	*Hit wall/Pole/Fastest lap*
ret	FRENCH GP	Paul Ricard	07/07/85	John Player Team Lotus	Lotus 97T-Renault	*Engine/Accident*
10	BRITISH GP	Silverstone	21/07/85	John Player Team Lotus	Lotus 97T-Renault	*Fuel injection problems*
ret	GERMAN GP	Nürburgring	04/08/85	John Player Team Lotus	Lotus 97T-Renault	*Cv joint*
2	AUSTRIAN GP	Österreichring	18/08/85	John Player Team Lotus	Lotus 97T-Renault	
3	DUTCH GP	Zandvoort	25/08/85	John Player Team Lotus	Lotus 97T-Renault	
3	ITALIAN GP	Monza	08/09/85	John Player Team Lotus	Lotus 97T-Renault	*Pole*
1	BELGIAN GP	Spa	15/09/85	John Player Team Lotus	Lotus 97T-Renault	
2	EUROPEAN GP	Brands Hatch	06/10/85	John Player Team Lotus	Lotus 97T-Renault	*Pole*
ret	SOUTH AFRICAN GP	Kyalami	19/10/85	John Player Team Lotus	Lotus 97T-Renault	*Engine*
ret	AUSTRALIAN GP	Adelaide	03/11/85	John Player Team Lotus	Lotus 97T-Renault	*Engine/Pole*

1986

2	BRAZILIAN GP	Rio	23/03/86	John Player Team Lotus	Lotus 98T-Renault	*Pole/Incident with Mansell*
1	SPANISH GP	Jerez	13/04/86	John Player Team Lotus	Lotus 98T-Renault	*Pole*
ret	SAN MARINO GP	Imola	27/04/86	John Player Team Lotus	Lotus 98T-Renault	*Wheel bearing/Pole*
3	MONACO GP	Monte Carlo	11/05/86	John Player Team Lotus	Lotus 98T-Renault	
2	BELGIAN GP	Spa	25/05/86	John Player Team Lotus	Lotus 98T-Renault	
5	CANADIAN GP	Montreal	15/06/86	John Player Team Lotus	Lotus 98T-Renault	
1	DETROIT GP	Detroit	22/06/86	John Player Team Lotus	Lotus 98T-Renault	*Pole*
ret	FRENCH GP	Paul Ricard	06/07/86	John Player Team Lotus	Lotus 98T-Renault	*Spun off on oil/Pole*
ret	BRITISH GP	Brands Hatch	13/07/86	John Player Team Lotus	Lotus 98T-Renault	*Gearbox*
2	GERMAN GP	Hockenheim	27/07/86	John Player Team Lotus	Lotus 98T-Renault	
2	HUNGARIAN GP	Hungaroring	10/08/86	John Player Team Lotus	Lotus 98T-Renault	*Pole*
ret	AUSTRIAN GP	Österreichring	17/08/86	John Player Team Lotus	Lotus 98T-Renault	*Engine*
ret	ITALIAN GP	Monza	07/09/86	John Player Team Lotus	Lotus 98T-Renault	*Transmission*
4	PORTUGUESE GP	Estoril	21/09/86	John Player Team Lotus	Lotus 98T-Renault	*Pole*
3	MEXICAN GP	Mexico City	12/10/86	John Player Team Lotus	Lotus 98T-Renault	*Pole*
ret	AUSTRALIAN GP	Adelaide	26/10/86	John Player Team Lotus	Lotus 98T-Renault	*Engine*

1987

ret	BRAZILIAN GP	Rio	12/04/87	Camel Team Lotus Honda	Lotus 99T-Honda	*Engine*
2	SAN MARINO GP	Imola	03/05/87	Camel Team Lotus Honda	Lotus 99T-Honda	*Pole*
ret	BELGIAN GP	Spa	17/05/87	Camel Team Lotus Honda	Lotus 99T-Honda	*Accident with Mansell*
1	MONACO GP	Monte Carlo	31/05/87	Camel Team Lotus Honda	Lotus 99T-Honda	*Fastest lap*
1	DETROIT GP	Detroit	21/06/87	Camel Team Lotus Honda	Lotus 99T-Honda	*Fastest lap*
4	FRENCH GP	Paul Ricard	05/07/87	Camel Team Lotus Honda	Lotus 99T-Honda	
3	BRITISH GP	Silverstone	12/07/87	Camel Team Lotus Honda	Lotus 99T-Honda	
3	GERMAN GP	Hockenheim	26/07/87	Camel Team Lotus Honda	Lotus 99T-Honda	
2	HUNGARIAN GP	Hungaroring	09/08/87	Camel Team Lotus Honda	Lotus 99T-Honda	
5	AUSTRIAN GP	Österreichring	16/08/87	Camel Team Lotus Honda	Lotus 99T-Honda	
2	ITALIAN GP	Monza	06/09/87	Camel Team Lotus Honda	Lotus 99T-Honda	*Fastest lap*
7	PORTUGUESE GP	Estoril	20/09/87	Camel Team Lotus Honda	Lotus 99T-Honda	*Pit stop/Throttle problems*
5	SPANISH GP	Jerez	27/09/87	Camel Team Lotus Honda	Lotus 99T-Honda	*Tyre problems*
ret	MEXICAN GP	Mexico City	18/10/87	Camel Team Lotus Honda	Lotus 99T-Honda	*Spun off*
2	JAPANESE GP	Suzuka	01/11/87	Camel Team Lotus Honda	Lotus 99T-Honda	
dsq	AUSTRALIAN GP	Adelaide	15/11/87	Camel Team Lotus Honda	Lotus 99T-Honda	*Oversize brake ducts*

1988

dsq	BRAZILIAN GP	Rio	03/04/88	Honda Marlboro McLaren	McLaren MP4/4-Honda	*Changed cars illegally/Pole*
1	SAN MARINO GP	Imola	01/05/88	Honda Marlboro McLaren	McLaren MP4/4-Honda	*Pole*
ret	MONACO GP	Monte Carlo	15/05/88	Honda Marlboro McLaren	McLaren MP4/4-Honda	*Hit barrier/Pole/Fastest lap*
2	MEXICAN GP	Mexico City	29/05/88	Honda Marlboro McLaren	McLaren MP4/4-Honda	*Pole*
1	CANADIAN GP	Montreal	12/06/88	Honda Marlboro McLaren	McLaren MP4/4-Honda	*Pole/Fastest lap*
1	DETROIT GP	Detroit	19/06/88	Honda Marlboro McLaren	McLaren MP4/4-Honda	*Pole*
2	FRENCH GP	Paul Ricard	03/07/88	Honda Marlboro McLaren	McLaren MP4/4-Honda	
1	BRITISH GP	Silverstone	10/07/88	Honda Marlboro McLaren	McLaren MP4/4-Honda	
1	GERMAN GP	Hockenheim	24/07/88	Honda Marlboro McLaren	McLaren MP4/4-Honda	*Pole*
1	HUNGARIAN GP	Hungaroring	08/08/88	Honda Marlboro McLaren	McLaren MP4/4-Honda	*Pole*
1	BELGIAN GP	Spa	28/08/88	Honda Marlboro McLaren	McLaren MP4/4-Honda	*Pole*
ret	ITALIAN GP	Monza	11/09/88	Honda Marlboro McLaren	McLaren MP4/4-Honda	*Accident with Schlesser/Pole*
6	PORTUGUESE GP	Estoril	25/09/88	Honda Marlboro McLaren	McLaren MP4/4-Honda	*Hit by Mansell/Pit stop*
4	SPANISH GP	Jerez	02/10/88	Honda Marlboro McLaren	McLaren MP4/4-Honda	*Pit stop/Pole*
1	JAPANESE GP	Suzuka	30/10/88	Honda Marlboro McLaren	McLaren MP4/4-Honda	*Delayed at start/Pole/Fastest lap*
2	AUSTRALIAN GP	Adelaide	13/11/88	Honda Marlboro McLaren	McLaren MP4/4-Honda	*Pole*

1989

11	BRAZILIAN GP	Rio	26/03/89	Honda Marlboro McLaren	McLaren MP4/5-Honda	*Pole*
1	SAN MARINO GP	Imola	23/04/89	Honda Marlboro McLaren	McLaren MP4/5-Honda	*Pole*
1	MONACO GP	Monte Carlo	07/05/89	Honda Marlboro McLaren	McLaren MP4/5-Honda	*Pole*
1	MEXICAN GP	Mexico City	28/05/89	Honda Marlboro McLaren	McLaren MP4/5-Honda	*Pole*
ret	US GP (PHOENIX)	Phoenix	04/06/89	Honda Marlboro McLaren	McLaren MP4/5-Honda	*Electronics/Pole*
7/ret	CANADIAN GP	Montreal	18/06/89	Honda Marlboro McLaren	McLaren MP4/5-Honda	*Engine*
ret	FRENCH GP	Paul Ricard	09/07/89	Honda Marlboro McLaren	McLaren MP4/5-Honda	*Transmission*
ret	BRITISH GP	Silverstone	16/07/89	Honda Marlboro McLaren	McLaren MP4/5-Honda	*Spun off/Gearbox/Pole*
1	GERMAN GP	Hockenheim	30/07/89	Honda Marlboro McLaren	McLaren MP4/5-Honda	*Pole/Fastest lap*
2	HUNGARIAN GP	Hungaroring	13/08/89	Honda Marlboro McLaren	McLaren MP4/5-Honda	
1	BELGIAN GP	Spa	27/08/89	Honda Marlboro McLaren	McLaren MP4/5-Honda	*Pole*
ret	ITALIAN GP	Monza	10/09/89	Honda Marlboro McLaren	McLaren MP4/5-Honda	*Engine/Pole*
ret	PORTUGUESE GP	Estoril	24/09/89	Honda Marlboro McLaren	McLaren MP4/5-Honda	*Collision with Mansell/Pole*
1	SPANISH GP	Jerez	01/10/89	Honda Marlboro McLaren	McLaren MP4/5-Honda	*Pole/Fastest lap*
dsq	JAPANESE GP	Suzuka	22/10/89	Honda Marlboro McLaren	McLaren MP4/5-Honda	*Excluded/Pole*
ret	AUSTRALIAN GP	Adelaide	05/11/89	Honda Marlboro McLaren	McLaren MP4/5-Honda	*Collision with Brundle/Pole*

1990

1	US GP (PHOENIX)	Phoenix	11/03/90	Honda Marlboro McLaren	McLaren MP4/5B-Honda	
3	BRAZILIAN GP	Interlagos	25/03/90	Honda Marlboro McLaren	McLaren MP4/5B-Honda	*Collision with Nakajima/Pit stop/Pole*
ret	SAN MARINO GP	Imola	13/05/90	Honda Marlboro McLaren	McLaren MP4/5B-Honda	*Wheel rim damaged by stone/Spun off/Pole*
1	MONACO GP	Monte Carlo	27/05/90	Honda Marlboro McLaren	McLaren MP4/5B-Honda	*Pole/Fastest lap*
1	CANADIAN GP	Montreal	10/06/90	Honda Marlboro McLaren	McLaren MP4/5B-Honda	*Pole*
20/ret	MEXICAN GP	Mexico City	24/06/90	Honda Marlboro McLaren	McLaren MP4/5B-Honda	*Puncture*
3	FRENCH GP	Paul Ricard	08/07/90	Honda Marlboro McLaren	McLaren MP4/5B-Honda	
3	BRITISH GP	Silverstone	15/07/90	Honda Marlboro McLaren	McLaren MP4/5B-Honda	
1	GERMAN GP	Hockenheim	29/07/90	Honda Marlboro McLaren	McLaren MP4/5B-Honda	*Pole*
2	HUNGARIAN GP	Hungaroring	12/08/90	Honda Marlboro McLaren	McLaren MP4/5B-Honda	
1	BELGIAN GP	Spa	26/08/90	Honda Marlboro McLaren	McLaren MP4/5B-Honda	*Pole*
1	ITALIAN GP	Monza	09/09/90	Honda Marlboro McLaren	McLaren MP4/5B-Honda	*Pole/Fastest lap*
2	PORTUGUESE GP	Estoril	23/09/90	Honda Marlboro McLaren	McLaren MP4/5B-Honda	
ret	SPANISH GP	Jerez	30/09/90	Honda Marlboro McLaren	McLaren MP4/5B-Honda	*Punctured radiator/Pole*
ret	JAPANESE GP	Suzuka	21/10/90	Honda Marlboro McLaren	McLaren MP4/5B-Honda	*Collision with Prost/Pole*
ret	AUSTRALIAN GP	Adelaide	04/11/90	Honda Marlboro McLaren	McLaren MP4/5B-Honda	*Accident/Pole*

1991

1	US GP (PHOENIX)	Phoenix	10/03/91	Honda Marlboro McLaren	McLaren MP4/6-Honda	*Pole*
1	BRAZILIAN GP	Interlagos	24/03/91	Honda Marlboro McLaren	McLaren MP4/6-Honda	*Finished with 6th gear only/Pole*
1	SAN MARINO GP	Imola	28/04/91	Honda Marlboro McLaren	McLaren MP4/6-Honda	*Pole*
1	MONACO GP	Monte Carlo	12/05/91	Honda Marlboro McLaren	McLaren MP4/6-Honda	*Pole*
ret	CANADIAN GP	Montreal	02/06/91	Honda Marlboro McLaren	McLaren MP4/6-Honda	*Electronics*
3	MEXICAN GP	Mexico City	16/06/91	Honda Marlboro McLaren	McLaren MP4/6-Honda	
3	FRENCH GP	Magny-Cours	07/07/91	Honda Marlboro McLaren	McLaren MP4/6-Honda	
4/ret	BRITISH GP	Silverstone	14/07/91	Honda Marlboro McLaren	McLaren MP4/6-Honda	*Ran out of fuel last lap*
7/ret	GERMAN GP	Hockenheim	28/07/91	Honda Marlboro McLaren	McLaren MP4/6-Honda	*Ran out of fuel last lap*
1	HUNGARIAN GP	Hungaroring	11/08/91	Honda Marlboro McLaren	McLaren MP4/6-Honda	*Pole*
1	BELGIAN GP	Spa	25/08/91	Honda Marlboro McLaren	McLaren MP4/6-Honda	*Pole*
2	ITALIAN GP	Monza	08/09/91	Honda Marlboro McLaren	McLaren MP4/6-Honda	*Pole/Fastest lap*
2	PORTUGUESE GP	Estoril	22/09/91	Honda Marlboro McLaren	McLaren MP4/6-Honda	
5	SPANISH GP	Barcelona	29/09/91	Honda Marlboro McLaren	McLaren MP4/6-Honda	
2	JAPANESE GP	Suzuka	20/10/91	Honda Marlboro McLaren	McLaren MP4/6-Honda	*Let Berger through last corner/Fastest lap*
1	AUSTRALIAN GP	Adelaide	03/11/91	Honda Marlboro McLaren	McLaren MP4/6-Honda	*Pole/Race stopped*

Formula 1 World Championship placings 1st–6th + Pole + Fastest lap

Races	1st	2nd	3rd	4th	5th	6th	Pole	Fastest lap
126	33	20	13	4	4	3	60	17

Formula 1 World Championship positions

1984	9th=
1985	4th
1986	4th
1987	3rd
1988	1st
1989	2nd
1990	1st
1991	1st

Other Motor Racing Championship wins
1981 RAC FF1600 Champion
1981 Townsend Thoresen FF1600 Champion
1982 Pace British FF2000 Champion
1982 EFDA FF2000 Champion
1983 Marlboro British F3 Champion